Contentment

Unlock the Power of Contentment: Discover the Secrets to a Fulfilling Life and Achieve Lasting Happiness with Proven Strategies, Inspiring Stories, and Practical Tools in this Comprehensive Self-Help Guide

Lance P. Richards

Contentment: Unlock the Power of Contentment: Discover the Secrets to a Fulfilling Life and Achieve Lasting Happiness with Proven Strategies, Inspiring Stories, and Practical Tools in this Comprehensive Self-Help Guide

Table of Contents

01: Introduction: The Importance of Contentment in Life

The pursuit of happiness is a universal goal for many people, but despite our best efforts, true contentment often eludes us. In our fast-paced, modern society, we are constantly bombarded with messages that tell us we need more, do more, and be more in order to be happy. But the truth is, happiness is not something that can be attained through external circumstances alone.

Contentment, on the other hand, is a state of mind that can be cultivated regardless of our external circumstances. It is the ability to find peace and satisfaction in the present moment, and to be grateful for what we have rather than constantly striving for more.

The importance of contentment cannot be overstated. Studies have shown that people who are content with their lives are more likely to experience positive emotions, have better physical health, and enjoy better relationships with others. They are also more resilient in the face of adversity, and are better able to cope with stress and difficult situations.

Yet, despite its many benefits, contentment is a skill that is

01: INTRODUCTION: THE IMPORTANCE OF CONTENT-MENT IN LIFE

often overlooked and undervalued in our society. We are conditioned to believe that success and happiness are synonymous with material wealth, status, and achievement. We are told that we should always be striving for more, and that contentment is a sign of complacency or laziness.

But the truth is, contentment is not about settling for less or giving up on our dreams. It is about finding joy and fulfillment in the journey, rather than focusing solely on the destination. It is about recognizing the abundance that already exists in our lives, and cultivating a sense of gratitude for what we have.

In this comprehensive self-help guide, we will explore the many facets of contentment and discover the secrets to a fulfilling life. Through inspiring stories, practical tools, and proven strategies, we will learn how to cultivate contentment in our daily lives, and unlock the power of this transformative state of mind.

Whether you are seeking greater happiness, inner peace, or a more fulfilling life, this guide will provide you with the knowledge and tools you need to achieve lasting contentment. So join me on this journey, and let's unlock the power

01: INTRODUCTION: THE IMPORTANCE OF CONTENT- MENT IN LIFE

of contentment together.

02: Defining Contentment: Understanding the Concept and its Significance

Contentment is a term that is often used to describe a state of being where one is satisfied with what they have in life. It is a concept that has been studied and discussed by philosophers, theologians, and psychologists for centuries. Contentment is an important aspect of human life, as it is closely linked to happiness and well-being. In this chapter, we will explore the concept of contentment, its significance in our lives, and what it means to be content.

Defining Contentment

The word contentment comes from the Latin word contentus, which means satisfied. It refers to a state of mind where one is satisfied with what they have in life, rather than always striving for more. Contentment is often contrasted with the concept of ambition, where one is always striving for more and is never satisfied with what they have. Contentment does not mean that one should not strive for more or set goals for themselves, but rather that they are able to find satisfaction and happiness in their current circumstances.

Contentment can be thought of as a combination of several different elements, including acceptance, gratitude, and peace. Acceptance involves accepting the things that one cannot change and focusing on the things that they can control. Gratitude involves recognizing and appreciating the things that one has in their life, rather than focusing on what they do not have. Peace involves a sense of calm and tranquility, even in the midst of difficult circumstances.

Significance of Contentment

Contentment is an important aspect of human life because it is closely linked to happiness and well-being. People who are content with their lives are generally happier and more satisfied than those who are always striving for more. Contentment allows individuals to appreciate the things that they have in life, rather than always focusing on what they do not have. It also helps individuals to cope with difficult circumstances, as they are able to find peace and acceptance in the midst of challenges.

Contentment is also important because it can lead to a more

fulfilling and meaningful life. When individuals are content with their lives, they are able to focus on the things that truly matter, such as relationships, personal growth, and making a positive impact on the world. They are less likely to be distracted by material possessions or status symbols, and more likely to find meaning and purpose in their lives.

Being Content

Being content involves several different elements, including acceptance, gratitude, and peace. Acceptance involves recognizing the things that one cannot change and focusing on the things that they can control. It also involves letting go of negative emotions such as anger, resentment, or envy. Gratitude involves recognizing and appreciating the things that one has in their life, rather than focusing on what they do not have. It involves cultivating a sense of appreciation for the people, experiences, and things that bring joy and happiness to one's life. Peace involves a sense of calm and tranquility, even in the midst of difficult circumstances. It involves cultivating a sense of inner peace and contentment, regardless of external circumstances.

Practical Strategies for Cultivating Contentment

02: DEFINING CONTENTMENT: UNDERSTANDING THE CONCEPT AND ITS SIGNIFICANCE

Cultivating contentment is a process that takes time and effort. Here are some practical strategies that can help individuals cultivate contentment in their lives:

Practice Gratitude: One of the best ways to cultivate contentment is to practice gratitude. This involves taking the time to reflect on the things that one is grateful for in their life. It can be helpful to keep a gratitude journal or to take a few moments each day to reflect on the things that bring joy and happiness to one's life.

Let Go of Negative Emotions: Negative emotions such as anger, resentment, or envy can be a barrier to contentment. It is important to learn how to let go of these emotions and cultivate a sense of acceptance and forgiveness. This may involve techniques such as mindfulness, meditation, or therapy.

Focus on Relationships: Building strong relationships with friends, family, and community can be a powerful way to cultivate contentment. These relationships provide a sense of connection and belonging, and can help individuals feel supported and valued.

02: DEFINING CONTENTMENT: UNDERSTANDING THE CONCEPT AND ITS SIGNIFICANCE

Set Realistic Expectations: Unrealistic expectations can lead to disappointment and frustration, which can undermine contentment. It is important to set realistic expectations for oneself and to focus on progress rather than perfection.

Practice Self-Care: Taking care of oneself is an important part of cultivating contentment. This may involve activities such as exercise, healthy eating, getting enough sleep, or engaging in hobbies and interests.

Live in the Present Moment: Cultivating contentment involves learning how to be fully present in the moment and appreciate the joys and beauty of life. This may involve mindfulness practices such as meditation or simply taking the time to appreciate the beauty of nature or the company of loved ones.

Find Meaning and Purpose: Cultivating contentment also involves finding meaning and purpose in one's life. This may involve exploring personal values, setting goals, or finding ways to make a positive impact on the world.

Conclusion

In conclusion, contentment is an important aspect of human life that is closely linked to happiness and well-being. Cultivating contentment involves a combination of acceptance, gratitude, and peace, and can lead to a more fulfilling and meaningful life. By practicing gratitude, letting go of negative emotions, focusing on relationships, setting realistic expectations, practicing self-care, living in the present moment, and finding meaning and purpose, individuals can cultivate contentment in their lives and unlock the power of lasting happiness.

03: The Connection between Contentment and Happiness: Debunking the Myth of Material Possessions

The pursuit of happiness is an innate human desire that transcends cultural boundaries and time. It is a concept that has been studied and discussed by philosophers, scientists, and self-help gurus for centuries. But despite the many different approaches and theories, one thing is clear: happiness is not found in material possessions.

We live in a consumerist culture that bombards us with messages that tell us we need more to be happy. We are taught that the key to happiness lies in the next big purchase, the latest gadget, or the trendiest fashion. But the reality is that material possessions provide only temporary pleasure, and once the initial excitement wears off, we are left feeling empty and unfulfilled.

This is where contentment comes in. Contentment is the state of being satisfied with what you have, rather than constantly striving for more. It is the ability to find joy and meaning in the present moment, rather than always looking to the future for happiness. And contrary to popular belief, contentment is not synonymous with complacency or settling for less. Rather, it is a powerful tool that can help you achieve lasting happiness and fulfillment.

There are many benefits to cultivating contentment in your life. For starters, contentment can help you reduce stress and anxiety. When you are constantly striving for more, you are in a perpetual state of wanting, which can lead to feelings of inadequacy, anxiety, and stress. But when you learn to be content with what you have, you can let go of those negative emotions and find peace in the present moment.

Contentment can also improve your relationships. When you are content with yourself and your life, you are less likely to rely on others for validation or to feel envious of their achievements. This can help you build stronger, more fulfilling relationships based on genuine connection and mutual support.

Furthermore, contentment can lead to greater success and achievement. When you are content with what you have, you are better able to focus on your goals and pursue them with a clear mind and a sense of purpose. You are less likely to be distracted by the constant desire for more and can instead channel your energy into achieving what truly matters to you.

So how can you cultivate contentment in your life? Here are some practical strategies to get you started:

Practice gratitude: Take time each day to reflect on the things in your life that you are grateful for. This can be as simple as appreciating a beautiful sunset or the smile of a loved one. By focusing on the good in your life, you can shift your mindset towards one of abundance and contentment.

Live in the present moment: Rather than constantly worrying about the future or dwelling on the past, try to stay present in the moment. This can help you appreciate the simple pleasures in life and find joy in the here and now.

Set realistic goals: While it's important to have goals and aspirations, it's also important to set realistic expectations for yourself. Don't strive for perfection or compare yourself to others. Instead, focus on what you can realistically achieve and find contentment in the process.

Practice mindfulness: Mindfulness is the practice of being fully present in the moment, without judgment or distraction. It can help you cultivate a sense of inner peace and contentment, even in the midst of a busy or stressful day.

Embrace simplicity: Rather than constantly seeking more, try to simplify your life and focus on the things that truly matter to you. This can help you find greater meaning and purpose in your life, and can lead to a greater sense of contentment.

In conclusion, contentment is a powerful tool that can help you achieve lasting happiness and fulfillment. While material possessions may provide temporary pleasure, they are not the key to a fulfilling life. By cultivating contentment in your life, you can find joy and meaning in the present moment, build stronger relationships, achieve greater success, and reduce stress and anxiety.

It's important to note that cultivating contentment is not always easy. It requires a conscious effort to shift your mindset and let go of the constant desire for more. It may also require making changes to your lifestyle, such as simplifying your possessions or letting go of unhealthy relationships.

But the benefits of contentment are well worth the effort. By learning to be content with what you have, you can find a sense of peace and happiness that lasts far beyond the temporary thrill of material possessions.

To further illustrate the connection between contentment and happiness, let's consider the stories of two individuals: John and Sarah.

John is a successful businessman who has spent his life striving for more. He has a beautiful home, a fancy car, and all the latest gadgets. But despite his success, he finds himself constantly stressed and anxious, always worrying about the next big deal or the next big purchase. He rarely takes time for himself or his family, and his relationships suffer as a result. Despite all his material possessions, John is far from content.

Sarah, on the other hand, is a schoolteacher who lives a

simple life. She has a modest home, drives an older car, and doesn't own many fancy gadgets. But she is content with what she has. She takes pleasure in the small things in life, like spending time with her family, reading a good book, or going for a walk in nature. She has strong relationships with her loved ones and feels fulfilled in her career. Despite not having many material possessions, Sarah is happy and content.

These stories illustrate the powerful connection between contentment and happiness. While material possessions may provide temporary pleasure, they do not guarantee lasting happiness or fulfillment. Contentment, on the other hand, can help you find joy and meaning in the present moment, build stronger relationships, achieve greater success, and reduce stress and anxiety.

In conclusion, if you want to unlock the power of contentment and achieve lasting happiness and fulfillment, it's time to let go of the myth of material possessions. Instead, focus on cultivating a sense of contentment in your life through gratitude, mindfulness, simplicity, and realistic goal-setting. With these strategies, you can discover the secrets to a fulfilling life and unlock the power of contentment.

04: The Benefits of Being Content: Achieving Inner Peace and Joy

Contentment is a state of being where one is satisfied with what they have, and they feel no desire for more. It is a state of inner peace and joy, which brings about a sense of fulfillment in life. Being content is not about being complacent or settling for less; rather, it is about appreciating what one has and living in the present moment. In this chapter, we will explore the benefits of being content and how it can bring about inner peace and joy in our lives.

The Importance of Inner Peace

Inner peace is the key to a happy life. It is a state of being where one is at ease with oneself and the world around them. Inner peace is not something that can be achieved overnight; it takes time, effort, and practice. However, the benefits of inner peace are immense. It helps us to cope with stress, anxiety, and depression. It also helps us to live a more fulfilling life and have better relationships with others.

The Benefits of Contentment

Increased Happiness

Contentment brings about happiness. When we are content, we are satisfied with what we have and are not constantly seeking more. We enjoy the present moment and appreciate the little things in life. This leads to a sense of joy and happiness that cannot be found in material possessions.

Better Health

Studies have shown that being content can lead to better health. When we are content, we are less likely to suffer from stress-related illnesses such as heart disease, high blood pressure, and depression. Contentment also leads to better sleep, which is essential for good health.

Improved Relationships

Being content can also improve our relationships with others. When we are content, we are more patient, understanding, and accepting of others. We are less likely to be judgmental or critical, which leads to better communication and more meaningful connections with others.

Increased Productivity

Contentment can also lead to increased productivity. When

we are content, we are more focused on the task at hand and less distracted by external factors. This leads to greater efficiency and effectiveness in our work and personal lives.

More Gratitude

Contentment leads to more gratitude. When we are content, we appreciate what we have and are grateful for it. This leads to a positive outlook on life and a greater sense of satisfaction with our accomplishments.

Greater Resilience

Being content also leads to greater resilience. When we are content, we are better able to cope with life's challenges and setbacks. We are more adaptable and better able to bounce back from adversity.

Practical Tips for Cultivating Contentment

Practice Gratitude

One way to cultivate contentment is to practice gratitude. Take some time each day to reflect on what you are grateful for. This can be as simple as appreciating a beautiful sunset or a warm cup of tea. By focusing on what we have, rather than what we lack, we can cultivate a sense of contentment in our lives.

Live in the Present Moment

Another way to cultivate contentment is to live in the present moment. Instead of worrying about the future or dwelling on the past, focus on the present moment. This can be as simple as taking a few deep breaths or paying attention to your surroundings. By living in the present moment, we can let go of our worries and anxieties and cultivate a sense of peace and contentment.

Practice Mindfulness

Mindfulness is another effective way to cultivate contentment. By practicing mindfulness, we can become more aware of our thoughts and emotions and learn to observe them without judgment. This can help us to let go of negative thoughts and cultivate a sense of peace and contentment.

Focus on What You Can Control

Finally, it is important to focus on what you can control and let go of what you cannot. When we focus on things outside of our control, we can become anxious and stressed. By focusing on what we can control, we can feel more empowered and cultivate a sense of contentment. This means letting go of the need to control everything and accepting that some things are beyond our control.

In Conclusion

Contentment is a powerful state of being that can bring about inner peace and joy in our lives. By cultivating contentment, we can increase our happiness, improve our health, strengthen our relationships, increase our productivity, and cultivate a greater sense of gratitude and resilience. There are many practical tips for cultivating contentment, including practicing gratitude, living in the present moment, practicing mindfulness, and focusing on what we can control. By incorporating these practices into our lives, we can unlock the power of contentment and discover the secrets to a fulfilling life and lasting happiness.

05: Contentment as a Habit: Making it a Part of Your Daily Life

Contentment is not something that can be achieved overnight. It requires time, effort, and commitment. It is a habit that needs to be practiced every day. This chapter will guide you through the process of making contentment a part of your daily life. You will learn about the benefits of cultivating contentment, practical strategies for incorporating it into your routine, and inspiring stories that will motivate you to keep going.

Benefits of Cultivating Contentment

Cultivating contentment has numerous benefits for your physical, mental, and emotional well-being. Here are some of the ways in which contentment can improve your life:

Reduces stress and anxiety: When you are content, you are less likely to worry about the future or regret the past. You are more focused on the present moment, which can help reduce stress and anxiety.

Improves relationships: Contentment can help you appreciate the people in your life and develop deeper connections with them. It can also make you more compassionate and understanding, which can improve your relationships with others.

Increases gratitude: Contentment helps you focus on what you have rather than what you lack. This can lead to increased feelings of gratitude and appreciation for the good things in your life.

Boosts self-esteem: When you are content, you are more likely to feel good about yourself and your accomplishments. This can boost your self-esteem and confidence.

Promotes overall well-being: Cultivating contentment can improve your overall well-being and quality of life. It can help you feel more fulfilled, happier, and more at peace with yourself and the world around you.

Practical Strategies for Incorporating Contentment into Your Daily Life

Now that you know the benefits of cultivating contentment, let's discuss some practical strategies for incorporating it into your daily life.

05: CONTENTMENT AS A HABIT: MAKING IT A PART OF YOUR DAILY LIFE

Practice gratitude: Start each day by thinking of three things you are grateful for. This can be as simple as a sunny day, a good cup of coffee, or a kind word from a friend. Focusing on the good things in your life can help you cultivate contentment and a sense of appreciation.

Practice mindfulness: Mindfulness is the practice of being present in the moment and paying attention to your thoughts and feelings without judgment. It can help you develop a greater sense of calm and contentment. Try practicing mindfulness for a few minutes each day by sitting quietly and focusing on your breath.

Focus on the present moment: Instead of worrying about the future or regretting the past, try to focus on the present moment. This can help you cultivate contentment by appreciating what you have right now.

Practice self-care: Taking care of yourself can help you feel more content and at peace. This can include things like getting enough sleep, eating nutritious food, exercising, and taking time to do things you enjoy.

Connect with others: Spending time with loved ones and

building meaningful connections can help you cultivate contentment. Make an effort to reach out to friends and family members, join a social group or club, or volunteer in your community.

Inspiring Stories of Contentment

Finally, let's explore some inspiring stories of people who have cultivated contentment in their lives.

Rachel, a single mother of three, struggled with feelings of stress and overwhelm. She started practicing gratitude by writing down three things she was grateful for each day. Over time, she began to feel more content and at peace with her life.

John, a retired businessman, struggled with feelings of restlessness and boredom. He started practicing mindfulness by meditating for a few minutes each day. This helped him develop a greater sense of calm and contentment, and he started to appreciate the simple things in life.

Maria, a college student, struggled with feelings of anxiety and self-doubt. She started focusing on the present moment by practicing mindfulness and taking time for self-care activities like yoga and journaling. This helped her cultivate a greater sense of contentment and self-acceptance.

Sarah, a busy executive, struggled with feelings of stress and burnout. She started prioritizing her relationships by making time for her family and friends. This helped her cultivate a greater sense of contentment and fulfillment in her life.

James, a retired veteran, struggled with feelings of anger and resentment. He started volunteering at a local organization that helped veterans, which gave him a sense of purpose and connection to others. This helped him cultivate a greater sense of contentment and peace with his past experiences.

These inspiring stories show that cultivating contentment is possible for anyone, regardless of their background or circumstances. By practicing gratitude, mindfulness, self-care, and connection with others, you too can unlock the power of contentment in your life.

Conclusion

05: CONTENTMENT AS A HABIT: MAKING IT A PART OF YOUR DAILY LIFE

Contentment is a habit that can be cultivated through daily practice and commitment. By focusing on the present moment, practicing gratitude and mindfulness, taking care of yourself, and connecting with others, you can unlock the power of contentment and achieve lasting happiness and fulfillment in your life. Remember that cultivating contentment takes time and effort, but the benefits are well worth it. Start incorporating these strategies into your daily routine, and watch as your life becomes more joyful and fulfilling.

06: Developing a Content Mindset: Shifting Your Focus to the Positive

Contentment is not just a state of being, it is a way of life. It is a mindset that requires a conscious effort to develop, nurture and maintain. It is easy to get caught up in the stress and chaos of everyday life, which can cause us to lose sight of what truly matters. We can become consumed with negative thoughts, worries and fears, which can lead to dissatisfaction and unhappiness. However, by cultivating a content mindset, we can shift our focus to the positive, embrace gratitude and find joy in the present moment.

Developing a content mindset is not an overnight process. It requires patience, persistence, and a willingness to change. The first step towards developing a content mindset is to recognize that happiness and contentment are not the same thing. Happiness is an emotion that comes and goes, while contentment is a state of being that is not dependent on external circumstances.

To begin cultivating a content mindset, start by practicing gratitude. Take a few minutes each day to reflect on the things you are grateful for in your life. This could be any-thing from your health, your family, your job, or even the small things like a warm cup of coffee in the morning or a beautiful sunset. By focusing on the positive aspects of your life, you can begin to shift your mindset away from negativ-ity and towards contentment.

Another important aspect of developing a content mindset is to learn to let go of things that are beyond your control. This can be difficult, especially when it comes to things that are important to us, such as our relationships or our ca-reers. However, by focusing on what we can control and let-ting go of what we cannot, we can reduce stress and anxiety, and find contentment in the present moment.

Learning to live in the present moment is also key to devel-oping a content mindset. We often spend too much time dwelling on the past or worrying about the future, which can cause us to miss out on the beauty and joy of the present moment. By practicing mindfulness and being fully present in each moment, we can find contentment in the here and now.

Another important aspect of developing a content mindset

is to surround yourself with positivity. This means surrounding yourself with people who uplift and support you, and avoiding negative influences. It also means being mindful of the media you consume, and choosing to focus on positive and uplifting content.

In addition to these strategies, there are also practical tools that can help you develop a content mindset. One of these tools is journaling. By taking the time to reflect on your thoughts and emotions, you can gain a deeper understanding of yourself and your mindset. You can also identify patterns of negativity or self-doubt, and work to reframe your thoughts in a more positive way.

Another useful tool for developing a content mindset is meditation. Meditation can help you quiet your mind, reduce stress and anxiety, and improve your overall sense of well-being. By practicing meditation regularly, you can cultivate a sense of inner peace and contentment that will carry over into other areas of your life.

Finally, it is important to remember that developing a content mindset is an ongoing process. There will be days when negativity and self-doubt creep in, but by consistently practicing gratitude, mindfulness, and positivity, you can overcome these challenges and continue to cultivate a sense of contentment in your life.

In conclusion, developing a content mindset is a powerful tool for achieving lasting happiness and fulfillment in life. By focusing on the positive, practicing gratitude, letting go of what we cannot control, living in the present moment, surrounding ourselves with positivity, and using practical tools such as journaling and meditation, we can shift our mindset towards contentment and embrace the joy and beauty of life.

07: The Power of Gratitude: Cultivating a Thankful Attitude

Gratitude is a powerful tool that can transform your life in profound ways. It is the practice of acknowledging the good things in your life and being thankful for them. When you cultivate a thankful attitude, you begin to see the world in a new light. You become more positive, resilient, and joyful. In this chapter, we will explore the power of gratitude and how to cultivate it in your life.

The Benefits of Gratitude

Gratitude has numerous benefits for our mental, emotional, and physical well-being. Research has shown that people who regularly practice gratitude experience the following benefits:

Increased Happiness: Gratitude has been linked to increased levels of happiness and life satisfaction. When we focus on the good things in our lives, we feel more content and fulfilled.

Reduced Stress: Gratitude has also been shown to reduce stress levels. When we focus on the positive aspects of our lives, we are less likely to get caught up in negative thinking patterns that can lead to stress and anxiety.

Improved Relationships: Gratitude can also improve our relationships with others. When we express gratitude towards others, they feel appreciated and valued, which can lead to stronger connections and more meaningful relationships.

Better Sleep: Gratitude has also been linked to better sleep quality. When we focus on the good things in our lives before bed, we are more likely to fall asleep faster and stay asleep longer.

Increased Resilience: Gratitude can also help us become more resilient in the face of adversity. When we focus on the good things in our lives, we are better able to cope with difficult situations and bounce back from setbacks.

Cultivating Gratitude in Your Life

Now that we understand the benefits of gratitude, let's explore how to cultivate it in our lives. Here are some strategies you can use to practice gratitude:

Keep a Gratitude Journal: One of the most effective ways to

cultivate gratitude is by keeping a gratitude journal. Each day, write down three things you are grateful for. These can be big or small things, such as a warm cup of coffee in the morning or a supportive friend.

Practice Mindfulness: Mindfulness is the practice of being present and fully engaged in the moment. When we practice mindfulness, we are more likely to notice the good things in our lives and appreciate them. Try incorporating mindfulness into your daily routine, such as by taking a few deep breaths before meals or pausing to appreciate nature on your daily walk.

Express Gratitude to Others: Another way to cultivate gratitude is by expressing it to others. Take time to thank the people in your life who have had a positive impact on you. This can be done through a handwritten note, a phone call, or a face-to-face conversation.

Use Positive Affirmations: Positive affirmations are statements that help you focus on the positive aspects of your life. Try incorporating positive affirmations into your daily routine, such as by repeating a mantra to yourself before bed or when you wake up in the morning.

07: THE POWER OF GRATITUDE: CULTIVATING A THANKFUL ATTITUDE

Volunteer or Give Back: Giving back to others can also help cultivate gratitude. When we help others, we are reminded of the blessings in our own lives. Try volunteering at a local organization or donating to a cause that is meaningful to you.

Practical Tools for Cultivating Gratitude

In addition to the strategies above, there are also practical tools you can use to cultivate gratitude in your life. Here are some examples:

Gratitude Jar: A gratitude jar is a simple and effective way to cultivate gratitude. Find a jar and some small pieces of paper. Each day, write down something you are grateful for and place it in the jar. Over time, the jar will fill up with positive messages that you can read whenever you need a boost of gratitude.

Gratitude Meditation: A gratitude meditation is a powerful way to cultivate gratitude. Find a quiet place to sit or lie down and close your eyes. Take a few deep breaths and focus on the feeling of gratitude. Visualize the people and things you are grateful for and allow yourself to feel the emotions associated with gratitude.

Gratitude Walk: A gratitude walk is a simple and effective way to cultivate gratitude. Take a walk in nature and focus on the beauty around you. Notice the colors, textures, and sounds of your surroundings. As you walk, think about the things you are grateful for and allow yourself to feel the emotions associated with gratitude.

Gratitude Board: A gratitude board is a visual representation of the things you are grateful for. Find a corkboard or poster board and decorate it with pictures, quotes, and other items that represent the things you are grateful for. Display the board in a prominent place and take time to reflect on it each day.

Gratitude App: There are numerous gratitude apps available that can help you cultivate gratitude. These apps allow you to track your gratitude practice, set reminders, and share your gratitude with others.

The Power of Gratitude in Action

When we cultivate gratitude in our lives, we open ourselves

up to a world of possibilities. We become more positive, resilient, and joyful. We begin to see the world in a new light and appreciate the blessings in our lives. Here are some examples of the power of gratitude in action:

Gratitude in the Workplace: Cultivating gratitude in the workplace can lead to increased productivity, job satisfaction, and employee engagement. When employees feel appreciated and valued, they are more likely to be motivated and committed to their work.

Gratitude in Relationships: Cultivating gratitude in relationships can lead to stronger connections and more meaningful interactions. When we express gratitude towards our loved ones, they feel appreciated and valued, which can lead to increased intimacy and trust.

Gratitude in Health: Cultivating gratitude can also have a positive impact on our physical health. Research has shown that people who practice gratitude have lower levels of stress and inflammation, which can lead to improved immune function and overall health.

Gratitude in Community: Cultivating gratitude in our communities can lead to a more positive and supportive environment. When we express gratitude towards our neighbors, coworkers, and fellow citizens, we create a sense of connection and belonging that can lead to a more cohesive and resilient community.

In conclusion, gratitude is a powerful tool that can transform our lives in profound ways. When we cultivate a thankful attitude, we become more positive, resilient, and joyful. We begin to see the world in a new light and appreciate the blessings in our lives. By using the strategies and tools outlined in this chapter, you can begin to cultivate gratitude in your own life and experience the many benefits that come with it.

08: Letting Go of Comparison: Overcoming the Urge to Compete and Compare

Comparison is a natural human tendency that starts at an early age. From childhood, we are constantly told to be the best in everything we do. Parents want their children to excel academically, sports coaches want their players to win, and society tells us that we need to have a successful career, a perfect body, and a happy family. All these expectations can lead to an unhealthy habit of comparison, where we constantly compare ourselves to others, judge ourselves harshly, and feel inadequate.

The problem with comparison is that it can lead to a host of negative emotions such as jealousy, envy, and resentment. It can also cause anxiety and depression, as we strive to meet unrealistic expectations and constantly worry about what others think of us. Moreover, comparison can make us lose sight of our own values and goals, as we try to conform to the expectations of others.

In this chapter, we will explore the concept of comparison, its negative effects on our well-being, and practical strategies to overcome it and cultivate contentment.

Understanding Comparison

Comparison is the act of measuring ourselves against others in terms of social, economic, and personal attributes. It is a natural human tendency that starts at an early age and continues throughout our lives. The problem with comparison is that it creates a hierarchy where some people are seen as superior and others as inferior. This hierarchy can lead to negative emotions such as jealousy, envy, and resentment, as we strive to meet unrealistic expectations and constantly worry about what others think of us.

Moreover, comparison can make us lose sight of our own values and goals, as we try to conform to the expectations of others. We may end up living a life that is not true to ourselves, just to fit in and be accepted by society.

Negative Effects of Comparison

Comparison can have a host of negative effects on our well-being. Some of these effects include:

Low Self-Esteem: When we constantly compare ourselves to

others, we tend to judge ourselves harshly and feel inadequate. This can lead to low self-esteem, where we doubt our abilities and worth.

Anxiety and Depression: Comparison can cause anxiety and depression, as we strive to meet unrealistic expectations and constantly worry about what others think of us.

Resentment and Envy: When we compare ourselves to others, we may feel resentment and envy towards those who we perceive as more successful or happy than us.

Lack of Gratitude: Comparison can make us lose sight of the good things in our lives and make us focus only on what we don't have.

Loss of Authenticity: Comparison can make us lose sight of our own values and goals, as we try to conform to the expectations of others. We may end up living a life that is not true to ourselves, just to fit in and be accepted by society.

Strategies to Overcome Comparison

Overcoming comparison requires a shift in mindset and behavior. Here are some practical strategies to help you let go of comparison and cultivate contentment:

Practice Gratitude: Gratitude is the practice of acknowledging and appreciating the good things in our lives. By focusing on what we have rather than what we don't have, we can cultivate a sense of contentment and reduce the urge to compare ourselves to others.

Define Your Own Success: Instead of relying on external measures of success, such as money, status, or fame, define your own criteria for success based on your own values and goals. This will help you stay focused on what truly matters to you and avoid comparing yourself to others.

Embrace Your Uniqueness: We are all unique individuals with our own strengths and weaknesses. Embrace your uniqueness and celebrate your individuality, rather than trying to conform to the expectations of others.

Stop Comparing Yourself to Others: This may seem easier said than done, but it's important to be aware of when you're comparing yourself to others and actively try to stop those thoughts. One way to do this is to practice mindfulness and observe your thoughts without judgment. When you catch yourself comparing yourself to others, acknowledge it and redirect your focus to something positive.

Focus on Your Progress: Instead of comparing yourself to others, focus on your own progress and growth. Set small goals for yourself and celebrate your achievements, no matter how small they may seem.

Surround Yourself with Positive Influences: Surround yourself with people who uplift and inspire you, rather than those who bring you down. Seek out positive influences such as mentors, friends, or support groups.

Practice Self-Care: Taking care of yourself is crucial in overcoming comparison and cultivating contentment. Practice self-care activities such as exercise, meditation, or creative hobbies that bring you joy and help you relax.

Seek Professional Help: If comparison is causing significant distress in your life, seek professional help from a therapist or counselor who can provide you with tools and support to overcome this habit.

Conclusion

08: LETTING GO OF COMPARISON: OVERCOMING THE URGE TO COMPETE AND COMPARE

Comparison is a natural human tendency that can have negative effects on our well-being. It can lead to low self-esteem, anxiety, depression, and resentment. Overcoming comparison requires a shift in mindset and behavior. By practicing gratitude, defining our own success, embracing our uniqueness, and focusing on our progress, we can let go of comparison and cultivate contentment. It's important to seek professional help if comparison is causing significant distress in your life. Remember, contentment is not about being perfect or having everything, but about finding joy and fulfillment in what you have and who you are.

09: Embracing Imperfection: Finding Beauty in Flaws and Mistakes

The pursuit of perfection is a common goal for many of us. We strive for perfection in our careers, our relationships, and our personal lives. We believe that perfection is the key to happiness, success, and fulfillment. However, the truth is that perfection is an unattainable goal. It is a myth that leads to frustration, disappointment, and unhappiness.

In this chapter, we will explore the concept of imperfection and how embracing it can lead to greater contentment and happiness. We will discuss the beauty of flaws and mistakes, the benefits of letting go of perfectionism, and practical strategies for cultivating a more accepting and content mindset.

The Beauty of Imperfection

The idea of imperfection can be unsettling for many of us. We associate imperfection with failure, weakness, and inadequacy. However, imperfection is a natural part of life. Nothing and no one is perfect, and that is what makes life interesting and beautiful.

09: EMBRACING IMPERFECTION: FINDING BEAUTY IN FLAWS AND MISTAKES

Think about some of the most inspiring stories and characters in literature and film. What makes them so compelling is their flaws and imperfections. It is their struggles and challenges that make them relatable and human. We connect with them because we see ourselves in their imperfections.

The same is true in our own lives. Our imperfections make us unique and interesting. They give us character and depth. Embracing our flaws and mistakes can lead to greater self-awareness, self-acceptance, and self-love.

Letting Go of Perfectionism

Perfectionism is a mindset that is characterized by a constant striving for flawlessness and an intolerance for mistakes and failure. It is a mindset that can lead to anxiety, stress, and burnout. When we are focused on perfection, we are not able to appreciate the beauty of imperfection.

Letting go of perfectionism is not easy, but it is essential for achieving greater contentment and happiness. One of the first steps in letting go of perfectionism is to recognize the negative impact it is having on our lives. We need to acknowledge that perfectionism is a myth and that it is preventing us from living a fulfilling life.

Another important step in letting go of perfectionism is to practice self-compassion. We need to be kind and understanding to ourselves when we make mistakes and experience setbacks. We need to remind ourselves that we are only human and that it is okay to be imperfect.

Cultivating a Content Mindset

Cultivating a content mindset is about shifting our focus from what we don't have to what we do have. It is about appreciating the present moment and finding joy in the small things. When we are content, we are not focused on perfection or the need to constantly improve ourselves.

One way to cultivate a content mindset is to practice gratitude. Gratitude is about acknowledging and appreciating the good things in our lives. It is about recognizing the beauty in the ordinary and finding joy in the simple pleasures.

Another way to cultivate a content mindset is to focus on experiences rather than things. When we are focused on acquiring material possessions, we are never satisfied. There is always something new and better to have. However, when we focus on experiences, we are able to appreciate the moment and create lasting memories.

Practical Strategies for Embracing Imperfection

Here are some practical strategies for embracing imperfection and cultivating a more content mindset:

Practice self-compassion. Be kind and understanding to yourself when you make mistakes and experience setbacks.

Practice gratitude. Take time each day to acknowledge and appreciate the good things in your life.

Focus on experiences rather than things. Spend time doing activities that bring you joy and create lasting memories.

Embrace your flaws and imperfections. Recognize that they are a natural part of life and that they make you who you are.

Accept that mistakes are a part of the learning process. View mistakes as opportunities to grow and learn, rather than failures.

Challenge negative self-talk. When you notice negative thoughts, challenge them with positive affirmations or re-framing the situation in a more positive light.

Practice mindfulness. Focus on the present moment and observe your thoughts and emotions without judgment.

Surround yourself with positive influences. Spend time with people who support and encourage you, and avoid those who bring you down.

Set realistic goals. Instead of striving for perfection, set achievable goals that allow for mistakes and setbacks.

Take care of yourself. Practice self-care by getting enough sleep, eating well, and engaging in physical activity that you enjoy.

By embracing imperfection and cultivating a more content mindset, you can unlock the power of contentment and achieve lasting happiness. It is not about achieving perfection, but about finding joy and fulfillment in the journey. Remember, life is not perfect, but it is beautiful in all its im-

09: EMBRACING IMPERFECTION: FINDING BEAUTY IN FLAWS AND MISTAKES

perfections.

10: The Art of Simplicity: Simplifying Your Life for More Happiness and Contentment

Introduction

The pursuit of happiness and contentment is a universal human desire. We all want to be happy and content, but the reality is that many of us feel stressed, overwhelmed, and unfulfilled. We live in a world that values material possessions, wealth, and success, and we often equate these things with happiness. However, research shows that material possessions and success alone do not bring lasting happiness or contentment. Instead, true happiness and contentment come from within, from cultivating a sense of peace, satisfaction, and fulfillment in life. In this chapter, we'll explore the art of simplicity, and how simplifying your life can lead to more happiness and contentment.

What is Simplicity?

Simplicity is the state of being uncomplicated, uncluttered, and free from excess. It is the art of living with less, focusing on what is truly important, and letting go of what is not. In a world that is constantly telling us to do more, be more, and have more, simplicity can be a powerful antidote to stress and overwhelm. By simplifying our lives, we can reduce the amount of mental and physical clutter we carry, create more space for the things that truly matter, and find greater peace, happiness, and contentment.

Why Simplicity Matters

Simplicity matters because it helps us focus on what is truly important in life. When we simplify our lives, we free up mental and physical space to pursue the things that matter most to us, whether it's spending time with loved ones, pursuing a passion, or simply taking time to rest and recharge. Simplicity can also help us reduce stress, increase our sense of well-being, and improve our relationships with others.

The Benefits of Simplicity

The benefits of simplicity are numerous and far-reaching. Here are just a few of the ways that simplifying your life can lead to more happiness and contentment:

Less stress and overwhelm: When we simplify our lives, we reduce the number of decisions we need to make, the number of possessions we need to manage, and the number of commitments we need to juggle. This can lead to less stress and overwhelm, and a greater sense of calm and peace.

More time and freedom: When we simplify our lives, we free up more time and space to pursue the things that matter most to us, whether it's spending time with loved ones, pursuing a passion, or simply taking time to rest and recharge.

Greater clarity and focus: When we simplify our lives, we can better focus on the things that matter most to us. We can clarify our priorities, set meaningful goals, and make progress towards the things that truly matter.

Improved relationships: When we simplify our lives, we can also improve our relationships with others. We can be more present and attentive in our interactions, and we can prioritize the people and activities that bring us joy and fulfillment.

Increased gratitude: When we simplify our lives, we can also cultivate a greater sense of gratitude and appreciation for the things we have. We can focus on what we have,

rather than what we lack, and find greater joy and contentment in the present moment.

How to Simplify Your Life

Simplifying your life is a process, and it can take time and
effort to achieve. Here are some practical strategies to help
you simplify your life and cultivate more happiness and
contentment:

Declutter your possessions: One of the most powerful ways
to simplify your life is to declutter your possessions. Take a
look at your belongings and ask yourself: do I really need
this? Does it bring me joy and fulfillment? If the answer is
no, consider letting it go. You can donate it to charity, sell it,
or simply throw it away. The less you have, the less you have
to manage, and the more space you have to focus on the
things that truly matter.

Streamline your commitments: Another way to simplify
your life is to streamline your commitments. Take a look at
your schedule and ask yourself: are there any commitments
that I can let go of? Can I say no to certain requests or invit-
ations? By reducing the number of commitments you have,

you can free up more time and mental space to focus on the things that matter most to you.

Prioritize self-care: Taking care of yourself is essential for simplifying your life and cultivating more happiness and contentment. Prioritize self-care activities like exercise, meditation, and spending time in nature. By taking care of yourself, you can reduce stress, increase your sense of well-being, and improve your relationships with others.

Focus on experiences, not possessions: Instead of focusing on accumulating material possessions, focus on accumulating experiences. Spend time with loved ones, pursue hobbies and passions, and travel to new places. Experiences can bring greater joy and fulfillment than material possessions, and they can create lasting memories and connections.

Practice gratitude: Finally, practice gratitude. Cultivate a sense of appreciation for the things you have in your life, whether it's your health, your relationships, or the simple pleasures of life. By focusing on what you have, rather than what you lack, you can cultivate greater happiness and contentment in the present moment.

10: THE ART OF SIMPLICITY: SIMPLIFYING YOUR LIFE FOR MORE HAPPINESS AND CONTENTMENT

Conclusion

Simplicity is a powerful tool for cultivating more happiness and contentment in life. By simplifying our lives, we can reduce stress and overwhelm, create more space for the things that truly matter, and find greater peace, happiness, and contentment. While simplifying your life is a process that takes time and effort, the benefits are numerous and far-reaching. By focusing on what is truly important, we can live a more fulfilling life and achieve lasting happiness and contentment.

11: Living in the Moment: Mindfulness Practices for Contentment

Living in the Moment: Mindfulness Practices for Contentment

Have you ever found yourself lost in thought, consumed by worries about the future or regrets about the past? We all have. It's part of being human. But when these thoughts start to take over our lives, it can lead to anxiety, stress, and a sense of discontentment. The good news is that there is a way to break free from this cycle and find contentment in the present moment. That way is through mindfulness.

Mindfulness is the practice of being present and fully engaged in the current moment, without judgment. It's a way of training our minds to focus on the here and now, rather than getting caught up in thoughts about the past or future. Through mindfulness, we can learn to appreciate the beauty of the present moment and find contentment in what we have, rather than always striving for more.

In this chapter, we'll explore the concept of mindfulness in more detail and provide practical tips and exercises to help you incorporate mindfulness practices into your daily life.

11: LIVING IN THE MOMENT: MINDFULNESS PRACTICES FOR CONTENTMENT

Whether you're new to mindfulness or an experienced practitioner, these techniques will help you find greater contentment and peace of mind.

The Benefits of Mindfulness

Before we dive into the techniques of mindfulness, let's first take a look at why mindfulness is so beneficial for our mental health and well-being.

Reduces Stress and Anxiety: Mindfulness has been shown to reduce stress and anxiety by helping us to focus on the present moment and let go of worries about the future or regrets about the past.

Improves Emotional Regulation: By training our minds to be present and non-judgmental, mindfulness can improve our ability to regulate our emotions and respond more effectively to challenging situations.

Enhances Cognitive Function: Mindfulness can also enhance our cognitive function, including attention, memory, and decision-making skills.

Boosts Happiness and Well-being: By cultivating a sense of

gratitude and appreciation for the present moment, mindfulness can boost our overall happiness and well-being.

Improves Physical Health: Mindfulness has been shown to have a positive impact on physical health, including lowering blood pressure, improving sleep, and reducing chronic pain.

Now that we understand the benefits of mindfulness, let's explore some practical techniques to incorporate mindfulness into our daily lives.

Techniques for Practicing Mindfulness

Mindful Breathing: One of the simplest ways to practice mindfulness is through mindful breathing. Simply take a few minutes to focus on your breath, noticing the sensation of the air moving in and out of your body. If your mind starts to wander, gently bring it back to your breath without judgment.

Body Scan Meditation: The body scan meditation is another powerful mindfulness technique. To practice this, lie down or sit comfortably and bring your attention to different parts of your body, starting at your toes and moving up to the top of your head. Notice any sensations or tensions in each part of your body, without judgment or analysis.

Mindful Walking: Walking can also be a great way to practice mindfulness. As you walk, focus on the sensation of your feet touching the ground, the movement of your body, and the sights and sounds around you. If your mind starts to wander, gently bring it back to the present moment.

Gratitude Practice: Another powerful mindfulness technique is to cultivate a sense of gratitude for the present moment. Take a few minutes each day to think about the things you're grateful for, whether it's the people in your life, the opportunities you have, or the beauty of nature around you.

Mindful Eating: Eating can also be a mindful experience. Take the time to savor each bite of food, noticing the flavors and textures. Avoid distractions like TV or phone calls and focus solely on the act of eating. This can help you develop a greater appreciation for the food you have and lead to a more mindful approach to nutrition.

Mindful Listening: Mindful listening involves paying attention to the sounds around you, without getting caught up in your own thoughts or judgments. Whether it's the sound of birds singing, the hum of traffic, or the voices of people around you, take a few minutes to simply listen and appreciate the sounds of the present moment.

Mindful Pause: Finally, taking a mindful pause throughout the day can help you stay present and focused. Set aside a few minutes at regular intervals to simply stop what you're doing and focus on your breath or the sensations in your body. This can help you reset and approach the rest of your day with a more mindful attitude.

Incorporating Mindfulness into Your Daily Life

Now that you have a better understanding of the benefits and techniques of mindfulness, how can you incorporate it into your daily life? Here are a few tips to help you get started:

Set aside time each day to practice mindfulness. Whether it's a few minutes in the morning or before bed, taking the time to practice mindfulness can help you stay present and focused throughout the day.

Use reminders to stay mindful. Set reminders on your phone or computer to take a mindful pause throughout the day or to practice mindful breathing.

Practice mindfulness in everyday activities. You don't need to set aside special time to practice mindfulness. You can incorporate it into your daily activities, such as while brushing your teeth, walking the dog, or doing the dishes.

Practice self-compassion. Mindfulness is about being present and non-judgmental. It's important to extend that same kindness and compassion to yourself, especially when you find your mind wandering or struggling with negative thoughts.

Find a mindfulness community. Joining a mindfulness group or attending a mindfulness retreat can help you stay motivated and learn from others who are also on the mindfulness journey.

Conclusion

Incorporating mindfulness practices into your daily life can help you find greater contentment and peace of mind. By focusing on the present moment and cultivating a sense of gratitude for what you have, you can break free from the cycle of worry and find lasting happiness. Whether you're new to mindfulness or an experienced practitioner, these techniques and tips can help you stay present and focused, and unlock the power of contentment in your life.

12: Understanding the Role of Expectations: How Unrealistic Expectations Can Sabotage Contentment

Introduction

Expectations are an integral part of human life. We all have expectations, whether conscious or unconscious, about ourselves, others, and the world around us. These expectations can be positive, serving as a source of motivation and hope, or they can be negative, leading to disappointment, frustration, and even despair. Therefore, understanding the role of expectations in our lives is essential to unlocking the power of contentment.

In this chapter, we will explore the nature of expectations, their impact on our wellbeing, and how unrealistic expectations can sabotage contentment. We will also provide practical strategies to help you manage your expectations, cultivate realistic ones, and achieve lasting happiness.

The Nature of Expectations

12: UNDERSTANDING THE ROLE OF EXPECTATIONS: HOW UNREALISTIC EXPECTATIONS CAN SABOTAGE CONTENTMENT

Expectations are mental representations of future events, experiences, or outcomes. They are based on our past experiences, beliefs, values, and desires. Expectations can be explicit or implicit, rational or irrational, realistic or unrealistic, and conscious or unconscious.

For example, if you expect to receive a promotion at work because you have worked hard and performed well, you have a rational and explicit expectation. If you expect to find love and happiness because you believe you deserve it, you have an implicit and unconscious expectation. If you expect to win the lottery and become a millionaire without buying a ticket, you have an irrational and unrealistic expectation.

Expectations can also be categorized as internal or external. Internal expectations refer to the standards, goals, and aspirations that we set for ourselves, while external expectations refer to the standards, goals, and aspirations that others set for us or that we perceive others to have.

The Impact of Expectations on Wellbeing

12: UNDERSTANDING THE ROLE OF EXPECTATIONS: HOW UNREALISTIC EXPECTATIONS CAN SABOTAGE CONTENTMENT

Expectations can have a significant impact on our well-being. Positive expectations can inspire us, motivate us, and give us hope for the future. They can also increase our sense of control and self-efficacy, leading to greater resilience and adaptability.

On the other hand, negative expectations can lead to disappointment, frustration, and despair. They can also undermine our sense of control and self-efficacy, leading to lower self-esteem and confidence.

Unrealistic expectations, in particular, can be harmful to our wellbeing. When we have unrealistic expectations, we set ourselves up for failure and disappointment. We may also engage in self-blame, self-criticism, and negative self-talk, which can further erode our self-esteem and confidence.

For example, if you have an unrealistic expectation that you should never make mistakes or experience setbacks, you will likely feel overwhelmed, anxious, and helpless when you do. You may also blame yourself for your perceived failures, instead of recognizing that setbacks are a natural part of growth and learning.

How Unrealistic Expectations Can Sabotage Contentment

Contentment is the state of being satisfied with what we have, who we are, and where we are in life. It is a sense of inner peace and fulfillment that comes from accepting ourselves and our circumstances, rather than constantly striving for more.

Unrealistic expectations can sabotage contentment in several ways. First, they can create a sense of perpetual dissatisfaction and restlessness. When we have unrealistic expectations, we are never satisfied with what we have or where we are in life. We are always striving for more, better, or different, which can lead to chronic stress and anxiety.

Second, unrealistic expectations can undermine our ability to appreciate and enjoy the present moment. When we are focused on what we don't have or what we haven't achieved yet, we miss out on the beauty and joy of the present moment. We may also take for granted the blessings and opportunities that we do have, leading to a sense of entitlement and ingratitude.

Third, unrealistic expectations can lead to a sense of inadequacy and self-doubt. When we have unrealistic expectations, we may feel that we are never good enough, smart enough, or talented enough to achieve our goals. We may also compare ourselves to others and feel inferior or envious. This can lead to a negative spiral of self-criticism and self-doubt, which can further erode our sense of self-worth and contentment.

Fourth, unrealistic expectations can strain our relationships with others. When we have unrealistic expectations of our partners, friends, or family members, we may become critical, demanding, or resentful. We may also project our own unmet needs and desires onto others, expecting them to fulfill us in ways that are unrealistic or unfair.

Fifth, unrealistic expectations can lead to burnout and exhaustion. When we have unrealistic expectations of ourselves, we may push ourselves too hard, sacrificing our health, wellbeing, and relationships in the process. We may also neglect our self-care needs, such as rest, relaxation, and play, leading to chronic stress and exhaustion.

Practical Strategies for Managing Expectations

Managing expectations is an essential skill for cultivating contentment and achieving lasting happiness. Here are some practical strategies to help you manage your expectations, cultivate realistic ones, and achieve greater wellbeing.

Practice mindfulness: Mindfulness is the practice of paying attention to the present moment with curiosity and non-judgment. When we practice mindfulness, we become more aware of our thoughts, feelings, and sensations, without getting caught up in them. This can help us recognize when we have unrealistic expectations and reframe them in a more realistic and compassionate way.

Cultivate gratitude: Gratitude is the practice of focusing on what we have, rather than what we don't have. When we cultivate gratitude, we become more aware of the blessings and opportunities that we do have in our lives, rather than taking them for granted. This can help us appreciate and enjoy the present moment, rather than constantly striving for more.

Set realistic goals: Setting realistic goals is an essential component of managing expectations. When we set goals that are achievable and meaningful, we are more likely to feel a sense of accomplishment and satisfaction. We are also more likely to experience a sense of control and self-efficacy, which can lead to greater wellbeing.

Practice self-compassion: Self-compassion is the practice of treating ourselves with kindness, understanding, and forgiveness, especially when we experience setbacks or failures. When we practice self-compassion, we are less likely to engage in self-blame, self-criticism, or negative self-talk. We are also more likely to bounce back from setbacks and maintain a sense of self-worth and contentment.

Communicate effectively: Effective communication is essential for managing expectations in our relationships with others. When we communicate our needs, desires, and expectations clearly and respectfully, we are more likely to build trusting and supportive relationships. We are also more likely to avoid misunderstandings, conflicts, and disap-

12: UNDERSTANDING THE ROLE OF EXPECTATIONS: HOW UNREALISTIC EXPECTATIONS CAN SABOTAGE CONTENTMENT

pointments.

Conclusion

Expectations are an integral part of human life, and they can have a significant impact on our wellbeing. Unrealistic expectations, in particular, can sabotage contentment, leading to chronic stress, anxiety, and dissatisfaction. However, by practicing mindfulness, gratitude, setting realistic goals, practicing self-compassion, and communicating effectively, we can manage our expectations, cultivate realistic ones, and achieve greater wellbeing and happiness. Remember, contentment is not about achieving everything we want, but about accepting and appreciating what we have, who we are, and where we are in life.

13: Practicing Self-Compassion: Accepting Yourself for Who You Are

As human beings, we all crave acceptance and love. Yet, many of us struggle with self-doubt, self-criticism, and a lack of self-compassion. We tend to judge ourselves harshly and compare ourselves to others, which can lead to feelings of inadequacy, low self-esteem, and even depression. However, practicing self-compassion can help us to accept ourselves for who we are, and ultimately, lead to a more content and fulfilling life.

What is Self-Compassion?

Self-compassion is the practice of treating ourselves with kindness, understanding, and forgiveness when we make mistakes or face challenges. It involves acknowledging our flaws and imperfections, but also recognizing our inherent worth and dignity as human beings. Instead of harshly criticizing ourselves for our shortcomings, we offer ourselves the same care and compassion that we would offer to a good friend.

Dr. Kristin Neff, a pioneer in the field of self-compassion, has identified three key components of self-compassion: self-kindness, common humanity, and mindfulness. Self-kindness involves treating ourselves with warmth, empathy, and understanding, rather than judgment and criticism. Common humanity involves recognizing that we are not alone in our struggles and that suffering is a natural part of the human experience. Mindfulness involves being present and non-judgmental, and accepting our thoughts and feelings without trying to suppress or control them.

Why Practice Self-Compassion?

Research has shown that practicing self-compassion can have numerous benefits for our mental and emotional well-being. For example, a study published in the Journal of Personality and Social Psychology found that self-compassion was associated with lower levels of anxiety and depression, and higher levels of life satisfaction and happiness. Other studies have found that self-compassion can increase resilience, reduce stress, and improve relationships with others.

Moreover, self-compassion can help us to break free from the cycle of self-criticism and self-doubt that can hold us back in life. When we are able to accept ourselves for who we are, flaws and all, we are more likely to pursue our goals and dreams with confidence and enthusiasm. We are also more likely to be kind and compassionate towards others, as we are no longer burdened by the weight of our own self-judgment.

How to Practice Self-Compassion

Practicing self-compassion is not always easy, especially if we have spent years or even decades being self-critical. However, with time and effort, it is possible to cultivate self-compassion and make it a part of our daily lives. Here are some strategies for practicing self-compassion:

Speak to yourself as you would speak to a good friend: When you make a mistake or face a challenge, try to speak to yourself with the same kindness and understanding that you would offer to a friend in the same situation. Instead of berating yourself for your shortcomings, offer words of encouragement and support.

Practice mindfulness: When you are feeling stressed, anxious, or overwhelmed, take a few moments to practice mindfulness. Focus on your breath and observe your thoughts and feelings without judgment. Remember that your thoughts and feelings do not define you, and that they are a natural part of the human experience.

Write a self-compassion letter: Write a letter to yourself, as if you were writing to a dear friend who was going through a tough time. Express your support, kindness, and understanding, and offer words of encouragement and hope.

Practice self-care: Taking care of yourself physically and emotionally is an important part of self-compassion. Make sure to eat nutritious foods, get enough sleep, exercise regularly, and engage in activities that bring you joy and fulfillment.

Cultivate gratitude: Practicing gratitude can help us to focus on the positive aspects of our lives, rather than dwelling on our flaws and shortcomings. Try to take time each day to reflect on the things that you are grateful for, no matter how small they may seem.

Seek support: It can be helpful to seek support from others when we are struggling with self-compassion. Talk to a trusted friend or family member, or consider seeing a therapist or counselor who can provide guidance and support.

Practice self-forgiveness: When we make mistakes, it can be tempting to dwell on them and beat ourselves up over them. However, practicing self-forgiveness can help us to move on and let go of our past mistakes. Remember that everyone makes mistakes, and that it is through our failures that we learn and grow.

Practice self-compassion daily: Finally, it is important to make self-compassion a part of our daily lives. Try to incorporate self-compassion practices into your daily routine, such as taking a few moments to meditate or write in a gratitude journal.

Conclusion

Practicing self-compassion can be a powerful tool for cultivating contentment and happiness in our lives. By treating ourselves with kindness, understanding, and forgiveness, we can break free from the cycle of self-criticism and self-doubt that can hold us back. While it may take time and effort to cultivate self-compassion, the benefits are well worth it. With self-compassion as our guide, we can learn to accept ourselves for who we are and live more fulfilling and content lives.

14: Fostering Healthy Relationships: The Impact of Positive Connections on Contentment

As humans, we are social creatures who thrive on healthy relationships. Our relationships with others play a crucial role in our overall well-being and contentment. Positive connections with friends, family, and romantic partners can have a profound impact on our happiness and fulfillment in life. In this chapter, we will explore the importance of fostering healthy relationships and the impact of positive connections on contentment.

The Importance of Healthy Relationships

Relationships are an essential part of human life, and they can take many forms. Some of us have close relationships with family members, while others develop strong bonds with friends or romantic partners. Regardless of the type of relationship, it is important to prioritize healthy connections with others.

Healthy relationships provide us with emotional support, encouragement, and a sense of belonging. When we have positive connections with others, we feel seen, heard, and valued. We also have someone to share our joys and sorrows with, which can enhance our overall sense of well-being.

On the other hand, unhealthy relationships can be toxic and draining. Negative connections with others can lead to feelings of loneliness, anxiety, and depression. When we feel unsupported or criticized by those we care about, it can damage our self-esteem and make it harder to find contentment in life.

Positive Connections and Contentment

Positive connections with others have a significant impact on our overall happiness and contentment. Studies have shown that people who have healthy relationships with others are more likely to report high levels of life satisfaction and well-being.

When we have positive connections with others, we feel more secure and less stressed. We have someone to turn to for emotional support and encouragement, which can help us overcome life's challenges with greater ease. Additionally, healthy relationships can help us develop a sense of purpose and meaning in life, as we are able to contribute to the well-being of others.

In contrast, negative relationships can have a detrimental effect on our contentment. When we feel unsupported or criticized by those we care about, it can lead to feelings of anxiety, depression, and low self-esteem. Negative connections with others can also drain our energy and leave us feeling depleted and unhappy.

Strategies for Fostering Healthy Relationships

Fostering healthy relationships takes time and effort, but it is well worth the investment. By prioritizing positive connections with others, we can enhance our overall sense of well-being and find greater contentment in life. Here are some strategies for cultivating healthy relationships with others:

Practice active listening: When we listen actively to others, we show that we value their thoughts and feelings. Active listening involves paying attention to what someone is saying, asking questions to clarify their point of view, and reflecting back on what they have said. This can help build trust and strengthen our connections with others.

Show appreciation: Expressing gratitude and appreciation for others can strengthen our relationships and enhance our sense of well-being. When we acknowledge the positive impact that someone has on our life, it can boost their self-esteem and foster greater connection.

Be vulnerable: Sharing our thoughts, feelings, and experiences with others can help build trust and deepen our connections. When we allow ourselves to be vulnerable with others, we create space for authentic connection and empathy.

Set boundaries: Healthy relationships require mutual respect and consideration. Setting clear boundaries with others can help us maintain healthy connections and avoid toxic dynamics.

Practice forgiveness: Conflict is inevitable in any relationship, but learning to forgive others can help us move past hurt and resentment. Practicing forgiveness can also help us cultivate greater empathy and understanding for others.

Conclusion

Fostering healthy relationships is a crucial component of contentment and overall well-being. Positive connections with others can provide us with emotional support, a sense of belonging, and a greater sense of purpose and meaning in life. By practicing active listening, showing appreciation, being vulnerable, setting boundaries, and practicing forgiveness, we can cultivate healthy relationships with those around us and experience the benefits of positive connections.

It's important to note that healthy relationships take time and effort to build, and not all relationships will be positive or beneficial for our well-being. It's okay to let go of relationships that are toxic or draining, and prioritize those that bring us joy and fulfillment.

In addition to cultivating healthy relationships with others, it's also important to cultivate a positive relationship with ourselves. Learning to practice self-care, self-compassion, and self-awareness can help us develop a stronger sense of self-worth and enhance our ability to connect with others in meaningful ways.

14: FOSTERING HEALTHY RELATIONSHIPS: THE IMPACT OF POSITIVE CONNECTIONS ON CONTENTMENT

In conclusion, fostering healthy relationships is a key component of contentment and overall well-being. By prioritizing positive connections with others, we can enhance our sense of happiness, fulfillment, and purpose in life. Remember to practice active listening, show appreciation, be vulnerable, set boundaries, and practice forgiveness, and enjoy the benefits of meaningful connections with those around you.

15: The Power of Forgiveness: Letting Go of Resentment and Anger

Forgiveness is a powerful tool that has the potential to transform your life. It is the act of releasing resentment and anger towards someone who has wronged you, and it can help you move past negative emotions and find peace within yourself.

But forgiveness is not always easy. It can be a difficult and painful process, and it may require you to confront painful memories and emotions that you have been avoiding. However, if you are willing to do the work, forgiveness can be one of the most transformative experiences of your life.

In this chapter, we will explore the power of forgiveness and provide you with practical tools and strategies to help you let go of resentment and anger, find peace within yourself, and achieve lasting happiness.

The Benefits of Forgiveness

Before we dive into the practical tools and strategies for forgiveness, it's important to understand the benefits of forgiveness. Forgiveness has been linked to a range of positive outcomes, including:

– Reduced stress and anxiety

– Improved emotional well-being

– Increased feelings of empathy and compassion

– Improved relationships with others

– Increased resilience and ability to cope with adversity

– Reduced risk of depression and other mental health problems

Forgiveness can also help you let go of negative emotions that may be holding you back in life. Holding onto anger and resentment can be draining and exhausting, and it can prevent you from fully experiencing the joys of life. Forgiveness can help you let go of these negative emotions and free up space in your life for more positive experiences.

The Process of Forgiveness

Forgiveness is a process, and it may take time to fully let go of resentment and anger. Here are some steps you can take to begin the process of forgiveness:

Acknowledge Your Feelings

Before you can begin the process of forgiveness, it's important to acknowledge and validate your feelings. If you have been wronged, it's natural to feel angry, hurt, or resentful. Take some time to sit with these emotions and allow yourself to feel them fully.

Understand the Other Person's Perspective

Try to understand the other person's perspective and what may have led them to hurt you. This can help you see the situation in a new light and may make it easier to let go of resentment and anger.

Practice Empathy and Compassion

Try to put yourself in the other person's shoes and practice empathy and compassion. This can help you see them as a human being with flaws and weaknesses, rather than a villain who intentionally hurt you.

Release Negative Emotions

15: THE POWER OF FORGIVENESS: LETTING GO OF RESENTMENT AND ANGER

One of the most powerful tools for forgiveness is to release negative emotions through journaling, meditation, or other forms of self-expression. This can help you process your feelings and let go of resentment and anger.

Make a Decision to Forgive

Finally, make a decision to forgive the other person. This may not happen overnight, and it may require multiple attempts. But the act of making a decision to forgive can be a powerful step towards letting go of negative emotions and finding peace within yourself.

Tools and Strategies for Forgiveness

Here are some practical tools and strategies you can use to facilitate the process of forgiveness:

Mindfulness Meditation

Mindfulness meditation can help you cultivate a sense of awareness and compassion towards yourself and others. It can also help you let go of negative emotions and find peace within yourself. Try incorporating a daily mindfulness meditation practice into your routine.

15: THE POWER OF FORGIVENESS: LETTING GO OF RESENTMENT AND ANGER

Gratitude Journaling

Gratitude journaling can help you focus on the positive aspects of your life and cultivate feelings of gratitude and contentment. It can also help you let go of negative emotions and shift your perspective towards forgiveness. Try writing down three things you are grateful for each day.

Cognitive Restructuring

Cognitive restructuring is a technique that involves identifying and challenging negative thought patterns. By challenging negative thoughts and beliefs, you can change your perspective and let go of negative emotions. Try identifying a negative thought pattern related to the situation you need to forgive and challenge it with a more positive and realistic thought.

Talk Therapy

Talk therapy, such as cognitive-behavioral therapy or psychotherapy, can be an effective way to work through the process of forgiveness. A therapist can provide a safe and supportive environment to explore your emotions, challenge negative thought patterns, and develop strategies for forgiveness.

Expressive Writing

Expressive writing involves writing about your emotions and experiences in a structured way. This can help you process your feelings and let go of negative emotions. Try writing about the situation you need to forgive, how it has impacted you, and what you can do to move forward.

Compassion Meditation

Compassion meditation involves cultivating feelings of compassion towards yourself and others. This can help you see the other person in a more empathetic and forgiving light. Try incorporating a daily compassion meditation practice into your routine.

Self-Care

Self-care is an important part of the forgiveness process. Make sure to prioritize your physical, emotional, and mental well-being by getting enough sleep, eating well, exercising, and practicing stress-reducing activities such as yoga or meditation.

Conclusion

Forgiveness is a powerful tool that can help you let go of negative emotions and find peace within yourself. While forgiveness can be a difficult and painful process, it is worth the effort. By practicing empathy, compassion, and self-care, and using practical tools and strategies such as mindfulness meditation, gratitude journaling, and cognitive restructuring, you can unlock the power of forgiveness and achieve lasting happiness. Remember, forgiveness is not just for the other person, it's for you too.

16: Finding Purpose and Meaning: Discovering What Matters Most to You

As human beings, we are wired to seek purpose and meaning in our lives. We crave a sense of direction, a reason for being, and a feeling of significance. When we have a clear sense of purpose, we are more motivated, more focused, and more content. We have a reason to get up in the morning and face the challenges of the day. Without purpose, life can feel meaningless and empty, leaving us feeling lost, anxious, and unhappy.

In this chapter, we will explore the concept of purpose and meaning, and how to discover what matters most to you. We will examine the benefits of having a sense of purpose, the obstacles that can prevent us from finding it, and practical strategies for uncovering your true purpose in life.

What is Purpose and Meaning?

Purpose and meaning are often used interchangeably, but they are distinct concepts. Purpose refers to our reason for being, while meaning refers to the significance or value we attach to our experiences, relationships, and accomplishments.

A sense of purpose gives us direction and helps us prioritize our goals and actions. It provides a framework for making decisions and navigating the complexities of life. Purpose can come from many sources, including our work, our relationships, our passions, and our spiritual or philosophical beliefs.

Meaning, on the other hand, is the emotional and psychological value we derive from our experiences. It is the feeling of fulfillment, satisfaction, and joy that comes from doing something that resonates with our values and beliefs. Meaning is subjective and varies from person to person. What is meaningful to one person may not be meaningful to another.

Why is Purpose Important?

Having a sense of purpose is essential for our overall well-being. Research has shown that people who have a clear sense of purpose tend to be happier, more resilient, and more satisfied with their lives. They are also more likely to experience positive emotions, such as joy and contentment, and less likely to experience negative emotions, such as anxiety and depression.

In addition to the psychological benefits, having a sense of purpose can also have physical health benefits. Studies have shown that people with a strong sense of purpose have a lower risk of cardiovascular disease, stroke, and cognitive decline in old age.

Obstacles to Finding Purpose

Despite the many benefits of having a sense of purpose, many people struggle to find it. There are several common obstacles that can prevent us from discovering our purpose, including:

Lack of self-awareness: If we don't know ourselves well, it can be difficult to identify our values, passions, and strengths.

Fear of failure: The fear of not living up to our own or others' expectations can prevent us from pursuing our dreams and discovering our purpose.

Cultural and societal expectations: We may feel pressure to

conform to societal norms or expectations, which can prevent us from pursuing paths that are truly meaningful to us.

Distractions and busyness: In our fast-paced world, it can be challenging to make time for reflection and introspection.

Strategies for Discovering Your Purpose

Fortunately, there are practical strategies that can help us overcome these obstacles and discover our purpose. Here are some steps you can take to uncover what matters most to you:

Reflect on your values: Take some time to consider what values are most important to you. These might include things like honesty, compassion, creativity, or justice. Once you have identified your values, think about how you can incorporate them into your daily life.

Identify your strengths: Consider what you are naturally good at and what comes easily to you. This might include skills like writing, public speaking, or problem-solving. Think about how you can use these strengths to make a difference in the world.

Explore your passions: Think about the things that excite and energize you. These might include hobbies, interests, or causes that you care deeply about. Consider how you can incorporate these passions into your daily life or pursue them more intentionally.

Reflect on past experiences: Think about moments in your life when you felt most fulfilled, engaged, or purposeful. What was it about those experiences that made them meaningful to you? How can you replicate or build on those experiences in the future?

Seek out new experiences: Try new things and explore new opportunities. This can help you broaden your perspective and discover new passions and interests. It can also help you develop new skills and strengths that you can use in pursuit of your purpose.

Connect with others: Seek out mentors, role models, or like-minded individuals who can offer guidance and support as you explore your purpose. Consider joining groups or organizations that align with your values and interests.

16: FINDING PURPOSE AND MEANING: DISCOVERING WHAT MATTERS MOST TO YOU

Practice gratitude: Take time each day to reflect on the things in your life that you are grateful for. This can help you cultivate a positive mindset and a greater sense of purpose and meaning.

Embrace uncertainty: Remember that discovering your purpose is a journey, not a destination. It is normal to experience uncertainty and doubt along the way. Embrace the process and be open to new possibilities and opportunities that may arise.

Conclusion

Finding purpose and meaning is essential for living a fulfilling and contented life. It can give us direction, motivation, and a sense of significance. However, discovering our purpose can be challenging, and there are many obstacles that can prevent us from finding it.

By reflecting on our values, strengths, passions, and past experiences, and by seeking out new opportunities and connections, we can uncover what matters most to us and pursue a life of purpose and meaning. With a clear sense of purpose, we can navigate life's challenges with greater resi-

lience and optimism, and experience a deeper sense of fulfillment and happiness.

17: Developing a Spiritual Practice: The Role of Faith in Contentment

Contentment is a state of mind that transcends material possessions and external circumstances. It is a deep sense of inner peace, satisfaction, and joy that comes from within. While there are many factors that contribute to contentment, including relationships, health, and personal achievements, one of the most powerful influences is faith.

Faith is a belief or trust in something beyond oneself. It can take many forms, including religious beliefs, spiritual practices, and philosophical convictions. Whatever form it takes, faith has the power to shape our attitudes, beliefs, and behaviors in profound ways.

In this chapter, we will explore the role of faith in contentment and how developing a spiritual practice can help us cultivate a deeper sense of inner peace, purpose, and fulfillment.

The Benefits of Faith

Research has shown that faith and spirituality can have a

profound impact on our physical and mental health. Studies have found that people who practice a religious or spiritual faith tend to have lower rates of depression, anxiety, and substance abuse, as well as greater resilience and coping skills in the face of adversity.

Faith can also help us find meaning and purpose in life. When we have a strong belief in something beyond ourselves, we are more likely to feel connected to a greater purpose and to find fulfillment in serving others and making a positive difference in the world.

Finally, faith can provide us with a sense of inner peace and contentment, even in the midst of difficult circumstances. When we trust in something greater than ourselves, we are better able to let go of our fears, worries, and anxieties, and to find a sense of calm and serenity in the present moment.

Developing a Spiritual Practice

If you want to cultivate a deeper sense of contentment in your life, one of the most effective strategies is to develop a spiritual practice. This may involve exploring your religious beliefs, practicing mindfulness and meditation, or engaging in other spiritual practices that resonate with you.

Here are some tips for developing a spiritual practice that can help you cultivate greater contentment:

Explore your beliefs: Take some time to reflect on your beliefs and values. Ask yourself what you believe in and what gives your life meaning and purpose. Consider reading books or attending workshops or classes that can help you deepen your understanding of your beliefs.

Practice mindfulness: Mindfulness is a practice of being present in the moment and paying attention to your thoughts, feelings, and sensations without judgment. Practicing mindfulness can help you cultivate a sense of inner peace and contentment by bringing your awareness to the present moment and reducing stress and anxiety.

Find a community: Connecting with others who share your beliefs and values can be a powerful way to deepen your spiritual practice and cultivate a sense of belonging and support. Consider joining a religious community or spiritual group, attending retreats or workshops, or participating in online forums or discussion groups.

17: DEVELOPING A SPIRITUAL PRACTICE: THE ROLE OF FAITH IN CONTENTMENT

Engage in acts of service: Serving others can be a powerful way to cultivate a sense of purpose and fulfillment in life. Consider volunteering your time and talents to help others, whether through your religious community or through other organizations that align with your values.

Seek guidance: If you are struggling to develop a spiritual practice or to find meaning and purpose in your life, consider seeking guidance from a spiritual mentor, counselor, or coach. They can provide you with insights, tools, and strategies to help you deepen your spiritual practice and cultivate greater contentment in your life.

Conclusion

Developing a spiritual practice can be a powerful way to cultivate greater contentment, purpose, and fulfillment in your life. Whether you explore your religious beliefs, practice mindfulness, engage in acts of service, or seek guidance from a mentor, the key is to find a practice that resonates with you and that helps you cultivate a deeper sense of inner peace and connection to something greater than yourself.

17: DEVELOPING A SPIRITUAL PRACTICE: THE ROLE OF FAITH IN CONTENTMENT

Remember that developing a spiritual practice is a personal journey and there is no one-size-fits-all approach. You may need to experiment with different practices and approaches until you find the ones that work best for you.

The most important thing is to approach your spiritual practice with an open mind and heart, and to be willing to explore new ideas and experiences. With time and commitment, you can cultivate a deep sense of contentment and inner peace that can sustain you through life's ups and downs.

In addition to developing a spiritual practice, it is also important to cultivate other factors that contribute to contentment, such as healthy relationships, fulfilling work, and good physical and mental health. By taking a holistic approach to contentment, you can create a life that is rich in meaning, purpose, and joy.

Ultimately, the key to unlocking the power of contentment is to cultivate a deep sense of gratitude and appreciation for the blessings in your life, even in the midst of difficulties and challenges. By focusing on the positive and practicing gratitude, you can create a mindset of abundance and joy that can sustain you through life's ups and downs.

17: DEVELOPING A SPIRITUAL PRACTICE: THE ROLE OF FAITH IN CONTENTMENT

In conclusion, developing a spiritual practice can be a powerful way to cultivate greater contentment, purpose, and fulfillment in your life. Whether you explore your religious beliefs, practice mindfulness, engage in acts of service, or seek guidance from a mentor, the key is to find a practice that resonates with you and that helps you cultivate a deeper sense of inner peace and connection to something greater than yourself.

Remember that contentment is not something that can be achieved overnight. It is a lifelong journey that requires patience, commitment, and a willingness to explore new ideas and experiences. But with time and effort, you can unlock the power of contentment and create a life that is rich in meaning, purpose, and joy.

18: The Connection between Physical Health and Contentment: Taking Care of Your Body

Contentment is a state of being that is characterized by a deep sense of satisfaction and happiness. It is a state of mind that is free from worries, anxiety, and stress. It is a state that everyone seeks, yet very few people achieve. Many people believe that contentment is something that can be achieved through material possessions or external circumstances. However, the truth is that contentment is a state that comes from within, and it is closely linked to our physical health.

The connection between physical health and contentment is undeniable. When we are physically healthy, we are better equipped to deal with the stresses and challenges of life. We have more energy, feel less fatigued, and are more mentally focused. In contrast, when we are physically unwell, we may feel sluggish, irritable, and find it challenging to concentrate. Poor physical health can also lead to chronic pain, which can have a significant impact on our mental health.

The first step towards achieving contentment through physical health is to adopt a healthy lifestyle. This includes eating a balanced diet, getting enough sleep, and engaging in regular exercise. Eating a balanced diet is essential for maintaining good physical health. This means eating plenty of fruits and vegetables, lean protein, and whole grains while avoiding processed foods, sugary drinks, and excessive amounts of alcohol.

Getting enough sleep is also critical for physical health. Most adults require between seven and eight hours of sleep per night. Lack of sleep can lead to fatigue, irritability, and impaired mental function. Additionally, getting enough sleep can help regulate hormones that control hunger, which can help with weight management.

Regular exercise is also essential for physical health. Exercise not only strengthens the body but also releases endorphins, which are natural mood boosters. Exercise can also help reduce stress levels and improve mental focus. It is recommended that adults engage in at least 150 minutes of moderate-intensity exercise per week.

Another critical aspect of physical health is maintaining a healthy weight. Being overweight or obese can lead to a range of health problems, including diabetes, heart disease, and certain cancers. Maintaining a healthy weight requires a combination of healthy eating and regular exercise.

In addition to adopting a healthy lifestyle, it is also important to take care of your mental health. Mental health and physical health are closely linked, and poor mental health can have a significant impact on physical health. Chronic stress, anxiety, and depression can weaken the immune system and increase the risk of developing physical health problems.

There are several strategies that you can use to take care of your mental health. These include:

Practicing mindfulness: Mindfulness involves being present in the moment and paying attention to your thoughts and feelings without judgment. Mindfulness has been shown to reduce stress and anxiety levels and improve overall mental health.

Practicing gratitude: Focusing on the things that you are grateful for can help shift your perspective towards the positive. Research has shown that practicing gratitude can lead to increased happiness and reduced stress levels.

Engaging in activities that you enjoy: Engaging in activities that you enjoy can help reduce stress levels and improve mental health. This could include anything from reading a book to participating in a hobby or sport.

Seeking professional help: If you are struggling with your mental health, it is important to seek professional help. This could include seeing a therapist or counselor, taking medication, or engaging in other forms of treatment.

In conclusion, the connection between physical health and contentment is significant. Taking care of your physical health through adopting a healthy lifestyle can help you feel more energetic, mentally focused, and less fatigued. Additionally, taking care of your mental health is equally important. Practicing mindfulness, gratitude, engaging in activities that you enjoy, and seeking professional help when needed can all help improve your mental health and overall sense of contentment. By taking care of both your physical and mental health, you can achieve a state of contentment that is not dependent on external circumstances.

18: THE CONNECTION BETWEEN PHYSICAL HEALTH AND CONTENTMENT: TAKING CARE OF YOUR BODY

It's important to note that achieving contentment through physical health is not a one-time event. It is a journey that requires ongoing effort and commitment. There will be times when you may slip up or fall off track, but it's important to get back up and continue the journey. Remember that every step you take towards improving your physical and mental health is a step towards achieving contentment.

One way to stay motivated and committed to your journey towards contentment is to set goals. Setting goals can help you stay focused and give you a sense of purpose. When setting goals, it's important to make them specific, measurable, achievable, relevant, and time-bound. For example, instead of setting a goal to "exercise more," you could set a goal to "exercise for 30 minutes, three times a week for the next three months." This goal is specific, measurable, achievable, relevant, and time-bound.

Another way to stay motivated is to track your progress. Keeping a journal or using a tracking app can help you monitor your progress towards your goals. It can also help you identify areas where you may need to make adjustments or seek additional support.

Finally, it's important to surround yourself with supportive people. Having a support network can help you stay motivated, provide encouragement, and offer accountability. This could include friends, family, or a support group.

In summary, achieving contentment through physical health requires adopting a healthy lifestyle, taking care of your mental health, setting goals, tracking progress, and surrounding yourself with supportive people. It is a journey that requires ongoing effort and commitment, but the rewards are well worth it. By taking care of your physical and mental health, you can achieve a state of contentment that is not dependent on external circumstances.

19: The Benefits of Nature: The Healing Power of the Outdoors

There is something inherently calming about being in nature, whether it's a walk in the park or a hike in the mountains. It is a well-known fact that spending time outdoors can have numerous health benefits for our mental and physical well-being. In this chapter, we will explore the healing power of nature and the many ways it can improve our overall quality of life.

Stress and anxiety are two of the most common mental health issues in our society today, and research has shown that spending time in nature can help alleviate these conditions. Studies have found that exposure to natural environments can reduce levels of the stress hormone cortisol, lower blood pressure, and improve mood. Nature has a calming effect on the mind and can help us feel more relaxed and at ease.

One of the reasons why nature has such a positive effect on our mental health is that it provides a break from the constant stimulation and distractions of modern life. The constant barrage of emails, social media updates, and notifications can be overwhelming, and taking a break from technology and spending time in nature can help us recharge and reset.

In addition to its mental health benefits, spending time in nature can also have a positive impact on our physical health. Being outdoors encourages physical activity, whether it's hiking, biking, or simply taking a leisurely walk. Exercise has been shown to have numerous health benefits, including reducing the risk of chronic diseases such as heart disease and diabetes, improving sleep, and boosting overall energy levels.

Another way in which nature can improve our physical health is through exposure to sunlight. Sunlight is an important source of vitamin D, which is essential for strong bones and a healthy immune system. Spending time outdoors can also help regulate our circadian rhythms, which can improve sleep and reduce the risk of insomnia.

Beyond its physical and mental health benefits, spending time in nature can also have a positive impact on our social lives. Studies have found that spending time in natural environments can increase feelings of social connectedness and improve social relationships. This is partly due to the fact that spending time outdoors encourages us to engage in activities with others, whether it's hiking with friends or joining a community gardening group.

In addition to its many health benefits, nature also has a powerful effect on our spiritual well-being. Many people report feeling a sense of awe and wonder when in the presence of natural beauty, such as a majestic mountain range or a stunning sunset. This sense of awe can help us connect with something larger than ourselves and provide a greater sense of purpose and meaning in life.

So how can we incorporate more nature into our daily lives? One simple way is to take a walk outside during our lunch break or after work. We can also plan weekend hikes or camping trips to get away from the hustle and bustle of city life. Even small changes, such as adding some plants to our home or office, can have a positive impact on our mental and physical health.

In conclusion, spending time in nature is one of the most powerful tools we have for improving our overall well-being. Whether it's reducing stress, improving physical health, or fostering social connections, the healing power of the outdoors is undeniable. By incorporating more nature into our daily lives, we can unlock the many benefits it has to offer and achieve greater contentment and happiness in life.

20: The Importance of Sleep: How Rest Can Improve Contentment

Sleep is a critical aspect of our lives that is often overlooked. In today's fast-paced world, many people prioritize work, social activities, and other obligations over getting enough rest. However, sleep plays a vital role in our physical and mental health, and neglecting it can have serious consequences.

In this chapter, we will explore the importance of sleep for contentment, discuss how rest can improve our overall well-being, and provide practical tips for getting better sleep.

The Benefits of Sleep

Sleep is a natural process that allows our bodies and minds to rest and recharge. During sleep, our bodies perform essential functions, such as repairing damaged tissues, boosting our immune system, and regulating our metabolism. Meanwhile, our brains consolidate memories, process emotions, and perform other critical tasks that help us function optimally during our waking hours.

Getting enough sleep can have a significant impact on our

overall health and well-being. Studies have shown that people who regularly get enough sleep are less likely to experience a range of health problems, such as heart disease, obesity, and diabetes. Additionally, getting enough rest can improve our mental health, including our mood, cognitive function, and ability to cope with stress.

The Relationship Between Sleep and Contentment

When we don't get enough sleep, it can have a significant impact on our overall contentment. Sleep deprivation can make us feel irritable, anxious, and stressed, making it harder to enjoy our daily activities and feel satisfied with our lives. Conversely, getting enough rest can improve our mood, boost our energy levels, and make us feel more content with our lives.

Additionally, sleep plays a crucial role in our ability to regulate our emotions. When we are sleep-deprived, our emotional regulation can suffer, making it harder to manage stress and cope with negative emotions. On the other hand, when we get enough rest, we are better able to regulate our emotions, leading to greater contentment and satisfaction.

20: THE IMPORTANCE OF SLEEP: HOW REST CAN IMPROVE CONTENTMENT

Practical Tips for Getting Better Sleep

If you're struggling to get enough rest, there are many practical strategies you can try to improve your sleep quality. Here are some tips to help you get better sleep:

Stick to a consistent sleep schedule. Try to go to bed and wake up at the same time every day, even on weekends. This can help regulate your body's internal clock and improve your sleep quality.

Create a sleep-conducive environment. Make sure your bedroom is dark, quiet, and cool. Use blackout curtains or an eye mask to block out light, and use earplugs or a white noise machine to drown out noise.

Avoid caffeine and alcohol before bed. Both caffeine and alcohol can interfere with sleep quality, so try to avoid consuming them before bedtime.

Limit screen time before bed. The blue light emitted by electronic devices can disrupt your body's natural sleep-wake cycle. Try to avoid using screens for at least an hour before bed.

Practice relaxation techniques. Engage in relaxation techniques such as meditation, deep breathing exercises, or yoga to help calm your mind and body before bed.

Exercise regularly. Regular exercise can improve sleep quality, but try to avoid exercising too close to bedtime, as it can interfere with sleep.

Consider seeking professional help. If you are still struggling with sleep, consider seeking help from a healthcare professional. They can help diagnose any underlying sleep disorders and provide treatment options to improve your sleep quality.

Conclusion

Sleep is a critical aspect of our lives that plays a vital role in our overall health and well-being. Getting enough rest can improve our mood, cognitive function, and ability to manage stress, leading to greater contentment and satisfaction with our lives. By prioritizing sleep and following these practical tips, we can improve our sleep quality and unlock the power of contentment.

21: The Role of Nutrition: Fueling Your Body and Mind for Contentment

The food we eat plays a crucial role in our physical and mental health. Proper nutrition can help us maintain a healthy weight, prevent chronic diseases, and improve our energy levels, mood, and cognitive function. In this chapter, we will explore the role of nutrition in contentment and provide practical tips for fueling our bodies and minds for optimal well-being.

The Importance of a Balanced Diet

A balanced diet is essential for overall health and well-being. It involves consuming a variety of foods from different food groups, including fruits, vegetables, whole grains, lean proteins, and healthy fats. A balanced diet provides the necessary nutrients our bodies need to function optimally, including vitamins, minerals, and fiber.

Eating a balanced diet can have a significant impact on our contentment. Studies have shown that consuming a diet rich in fruits, vegetables, and whole grains can improve our mood and reduce symptoms of depression and anxiety. Additionally, eating a balanced diet can improve our energy levels, making it easier to enjoy our daily activities and feel satisfied with our lives.

The Role of Macronutrients in Contentment

Macronutrients are the three main types of nutrients our bodies need to function properly: carbohydrates, proteins, and fats. Each macronutrient plays a unique role in our physical and mental health, and consuming them in the right proportions can help us maintain optimal well-being.

Carbohydrates provide our bodies with energy, making them essential for maintaining proper cognitive function and mood. Complex carbohydrates, such as whole grains, fruits, and vegetables, are a healthier choice than refined carbohydrates, such as white bread and sugar, as they provide a steady source of energy and are more nutrient-dense.

Proteins are essential for building and repairing tissues in our bodies, including muscle, bone, and skin. Consuming adequate amounts of protein can help us maintain a healthy weight, improve our muscle mass and strength, and promote feelings of fullness and satisfaction.

Fats are an essential nutrient that plays a critical role in our physical and mental health. They provide our bodies with energy, help us absorb important vitamins and minerals, and support brain function. However, it's important to choose healthy fats, such as those found in nuts, seeds, and fish, over unhealthy fats, such as those found in processed foods and fried foods.

Practical Tips for Eating a Balanced Diet

Eating a balanced diet can seem overwhelming, but there are many practical tips you can follow to make it easier. Here are some tips to help you fuel your body and mind for optimal well-being:

Fill half your plate with fruits and vegetables. Aim to consume at least five servings of fruits and vegetables per day, and choose a variety of colors to ensure you're getting a wide range of nutrients.

Choose whole grains over refined grains. Whole grains, such as brown rice, quinoa, and whole wheat bread, are more nutrient-dense and provide a steady source of energy.

Consume lean proteins. Choose lean sources of protein, such as chicken, fish, and legumes, over red meat and processed meats.

Incorporate healthy fats into your diet. Choose healthy fats, such as those found in nuts, seeds, avocados, and fish, over unhealthy fats, such as those found in fried foods and processed snacks.

Limit your intake of sugar and processed foods. These foods provide little nutritional value and can contribute to weight gain and other health problems.

Stay hydrated. Aim to drink at least eight cups of water per day, and choose water over sugary drinks.

Listen to your body. Pay attention to your hunger and fullness cues, and eat when you're hungry and stop when you're full.

Conclusion

Proper nutrition is essential for contentment and overall

well-being. Eating a balanced diet can improve our energy levels, mood, and cognitive function, and reduce the risk of chronic diseases. By consuming a variety of foods from different food groups and choosing healthy sources of macronutrients, we can fuel our bodies and minds for optimal performance and contentment.

In addition to following a balanced diet, it's important to be mindful of our eating habits. Mindful eating involves paying attention to the sensory experience of eating, including the taste, texture, and smell of food, as well as our hunger and fullness cues. By practicing mindful eating, we can enjoy our food more fully, make healthier food choices, and develop a more positive relationship with food.

It's also important to note that everyone's nutritional needs are unique. Factors such as age, gender, activity level, and health status can all influence our nutritional requirements. If you have specific nutritional concerns or health conditions, it's important to consult with a healthcare provider or registered dietitian to develop a personalized nutrition plan.

In summary, nutrition plays a crucial role in contentment and overall well-being. By following a balanced diet, choos-

ing healthy sources of macronutrients, and practicing mindful eating, we can fuel our bodies and minds for optimal
performance and contentment.

22: Coping with Stress: Managing Anxiety and Overwhelm

Stress is an inevitable part of life, and it can come in many forms: work-related stress, financial stress, relationship stress, and more. While a little stress can be motivating, too much stress can be overwhelming and detrimental to our mental and physical health. In this chapter, we will explore some proven strategies for coping with stress, managing anxiety, and finding contentment even in the midst of challenging situations.

The first step in coping with stress is recognizing the signs that we are under stress. Common symptoms of stress include irritability, mood swings, difficulty concentrating, insomnia, headaches, and physical tension in the body. Once we recognize these symptoms, we can start taking steps to reduce stress and manage our anxiety.

One of the most effective ways to cope with stress is through relaxation techniques. These can include deep breathing exercises, meditation, yoga, or other mindfulness practices. By focusing our attention on the present moment and letting go of worries about the past or future, we can reduce our anxiety and cultivate a sense of calm.

Another key strategy for managing stress is to prioritize self-care. This can include getting enough sleep, eating a healthy diet, exercising regularly, and taking time for activities that we enjoy. When we take care of ourselves, we are better equipped to handle the challenges that come our way.

In addition to these individual strategies, it can also be helpful to seek support from others. This might involve talking to a trusted friend or family member, seeking therapy or counseling, or joining a support group. By connecting with others who understand our experiences, we can feel less alone and more supported in our journey towards contentment.

One important tool for managing stress and anxiety is cognitive-behavioral therapy (CBT). This type of therapy helps individuals identify and challenge negative thought patterns that contribute to anxiety and stress. By learning to reframe our thoughts and beliefs, we can reduce our anxiety and feel more empowered to cope with challenging situations.

Another powerful tool for managing stress is to cultivate gratitude. Research has shown that practicing gratitude can increase happiness and reduce stress levels. This can involve keeping a gratitude journal, regularly expressing thanks to those around us, or simply taking time to appreciate the small things in life.

Ultimately, the key to managing stress and finding contentment is to cultivate a sense of inner peace and acceptance. This involves accepting ourselves and our circumstances, even when they are less than ideal. By focusing on what we can control and letting go of what we cannot, we can find a greater sense of peace and contentment in our lives.

To summarize, coping with stress and managing anxiety involves a combination of relaxation techniques, self-care, social support, cognitive-behavioral therapy, and gratitude practices. By incorporating these strategies into our daily lives, we can reduce stress, increase happiness, and unlock the power of contentment.

23: Overcoming Adversity: Finding Strength in Tough Times

Life is full of ups and downs, and we all face adversity at some point in our lives. Whether it's a challenging career, a difficult relationship, or a health crisis, adversity can test us and push us to our limits. But it's how we respond to adversity that ultimately determines our character and our success in life.

In this chapter, we'll explore the power of contentment in overcoming adversity. We'll share inspiring stories of people who have faced significant challenges and emerged stronger, and we'll provide practical strategies and tools for cultivating contentment in the face of adversity.

The Importance of Contentment in Adversity

When faced with adversity, it's easy to fall into a pattern of negativity and despair. We may feel overwhelmed by our circumstances, powerless to change them, and hopeless about the future. But cultivating contentment in the face of adversity can help us shift our perspective, find meaning and purpose in our challenges, and develop the resilience we need to overcome them.

23: OVERCOMING ADVERSITY: FINDING STRENGTH IN TOUGH TIMES

Contentment is the state of being satisfied with what we have, even in the midst of difficulties. It's not about ignoring or minimizing our challenges, but about finding peace and acceptance in the present moment, even as we work toward a better future. Contentment can help us stay grounded and focused, and it can give us the strength and courage we need to face our challenges head-on.

In order to cultivate contentment in the face of adversity, it's important to develop a growth mindset. A growth mindset is the belief that we can learn and grow from our challenges, and that our failures and setbacks are opportunities for growth and development. With a growth mindset, we can approach adversity as a chance to learn, to become stronger, and to develop new skills and abilities.

Finding Strength in Adversity

One of the most powerful ways to cultivate contentment in the face of adversity is to find strength in our challenges. Adversity can be a powerful teacher, helping us develop resilience, perseverance, and inner strength. By embracing our challenges and facing them with courage and determination, we can develop a deeper sense of self-awareness and self-confidence, and we can become more resilient and adaptable in the face of future challenges.

There are many inspiring stories of people who have found strength in adversity. Take the example of Malala Yousafzai, the young Pakistani activist who was shot in the head by the Taliban for advocating for girls' education. Despite this horrific attack, Malala refused to be silenced. She continued to speak out for women's rights and education, and she went on to become the youngest-ever Nobel Peace Prize laureate. Through her courage and resilience, Malala has inspired millions of people around the world to stand up for their rights and fight for a better future.

Another example is Nick Vujicic, a man born without arms or legs who has become a motivational speaker, author, and disability rights advocate. Despite the challenges he faces every day, Nick has found a way to live a fulfilling and meaningful life. He has traveled the world sharing his story of resilience and hope, and he has inspired countless people to overcome their own challenges and find strength in adversity.

These stories remind us that we all have the potential to

find strength and resilience in the face of adversity. By focusing on our strengths, embracing our challenges, and cultivating a growth mindset, we can develop the resilience and courage we need to overcome any obstacle.

Practical Strategies for Cultivating Contentment in Adversity

While finding strength in adversity is a powerful way to cultivate contentment, there are also many practical strategies and tools we can use to develop contentment in the face of adversity. Here are some of the most effective strategies:

Practice mindfulness. Mindfulness is the practice of being present in the moment, without judgment or distraction. When faced with adversity, mindfulness can help us stay grounded and focused on the present moment, rather than getting lost in worries and fears about the future. By practicing mindfulness regularly, we can learn to accept our challenges with greater ease and find peace and contentment in the present moment.

Cultivate gratitude. Gratitude is the practice of focusing on the good things in our lives, even in the midst of difficulties.

23: OVERCOMING ADVERSITY: FINDING STRENGTH IN TOUGH TIMES

By taking time each day to reflect on the things we're grateful for, we can shift our focus away from our challenges and toward the positive aspects of our lives. This can help us cultivate contentment and find joy and meaning even in difficult times.

Build a support system. When facing adversity, it's important to have a strong support system of friends, family, and professionals who can provide emotional support, practical advice, and encouragement. By building a support system, we can feel less alone and more empowered to face our challenges with strength and resilience.

Practice self-care. Self-care is the practice of taking care of our physical, emotional, and mental health. When facing adversity, self-care is especially important. By getting enough sleep, eating healthy foods, exercising regularly, and practicing stress-reducing activities like meditation and yoga, we can build our resilience and cultivate contentment even in the face of difficult circumstances.

Focus on what you can control. When facing adversity, it's easy to feel overwhelmed by the things we can't control. However, by focusing on the things we can control, we can feel more empowered and capable of creating positive change in our lives. By setting goals, taking action, and focusing on small, manageable steps, we can move forward with greater confidence and contentment.

Conclusion

Adversity is a natural part of life, but it doesn't have to define us. By cultivating contentment in the face of adversity, we can find strength, resilience, and joy even in difficult times. Whether we're facing a challenging career, a difficult relationship, or a health crisis, we have the power to overcome our challenges and create a fulfilling and meaningful life. By practicing mindfulness, gratitude, self-care, and focusing on what we can control, we can develop the resilience and courage we need to face any obstacle. So let's embrace our challenges, find strength in adversity, and unlock the power of contentment to achieve lasting happiness and fulfillment in our lives.

24: Dealing with Loss and Grief: Navigating Pain and Finding Comfort

Loss and grief are inevitable parts of the human experience. Whether it's the loss of a loved one, a job, a relationship, or a dream, the pain and sadness that come with it can be overwhelming. But there are ways to navigate the complex emotions that accompany loss and find comfort in the midst of sorrow.

The first step in dealing with loss and grief is to acknowledge and accept your feelings. It's natural to feel a wide range of emotions after a loss, including sadness, anger, guilt, and even relief. It's important to allow yourself to feel these emotions without judgment or shame. Don't try to suppress or ignore your feelings, as this will only prolong the grieving process.

Instead, give yourself permission to feel and express your emotions in a healthy way. This could mean talking to a trusted friend or family member, writing in a journal, or seeking the help of a professional therapist or counselor. Remember that there is no right or wrong way to grieve, and everyone experiences loss differently.

As you navigate your grief, it's important to take care of yourself both physically and emotionally. This means eating a healthy diet, getting regular exercise, and getting enough sleep. It also means giving yourself time to rest and relax, and engaging in activities that bring you joy and comfort.

One powerful tool for dealing with loss and grief is mindfulness. Mindfulness is the practice of being fully present in the moment, without judgment or distraction. It can help you stay grounded and centered in the midst of difficult emotions, and allow you to find peace and comfort even in the midst of pain.

To practice mindfulness, try focusing on your breath for a few minutes each day. Pay attention to the sensation of the air moving in and out of your body, and let your thoughts and emotions pass by without judgment. You can also try other mindfulness practices, such as yoga, meditation, or walking in nature.

Another important aspect of dealing with loss and grief is finding meaning and purpose in your life. This can involve setting new goals, exploring new hobbies and interests, or finding ways to give back to your community. It's important to remember that life goes on, and that you can still find happiness and fulfillment even in the midst of loss.

Finally, it's important to seek support from others as you navigate your grief. This may mean reaching out to family and friends, joining a support group, or seeking the help of a professional counselor or therapist. Remember that you don't have to go through this process alone, and that there are people who care about you and want to help.

In conclusion, dealing with loss and grief is never easy, but it is possible to find comfort and healing in the midst of pain. By acknowledging and accepting your feelings, taking care of yourself both physically and emotionally, practicing mindfulness, finding meaning and purpose in your life, and seeking support from others, you can navigate the complex emotions of grief and move towards a place of contentment and peace.

25: The Impact of Media and Technology: The Role of Social Media in Contentment

In the digital age, media and technology have become an integral part of our lives. Social media platforms such as Facebook, Twitter, Instagram, and Snapchat have revolutionized the way we communicate, connect, and share information. While these platforms have undoubtedly brought many benefits, they have also had a profound impact on our sense of contentment and well-being.

Social media has created a culture of comparison, where we are constantly bombarded with images of other people's seemingly perfect lives. This can lead to feelings of inadequacy and low self-esteem, as we compare ourselves to others and feel that we don't measure up. We see pictures of our friends on exotic vacations, attending glamorous events, or posting pictures of their new homes, cars, or gadgets, and it can be difficult not to feel envious or left out.

The constant stream of information and notifications on social media can also be overwhelming and exhausting. We feel pressure to stay connected and up-to-date, even when it's not necessarily in our best interest. Studies have shown that social media use is associated with higher levels of stress, anxiety, and depression, as well as decreased well-being and life satisfaction.

But social media is not all bad. It can also provide a sense of community and support, as we connect with others who share our interests, values, and experiences. We can find inspiration, motivation, and encouragement from others who have overcome challenges or achieved their goals. Social media can also be a powerful tool for social change, as we raise awareness and advocate for causes we care about.

The key to using social media in a way that promotes contentment and well-being is to be mindful and intentional about our use. We can set boundaries around our social media use, such as limiting the amount of time we spend on these platforms or taking regular breaks from them. We can also curate our social media feeds to include content that is positive, inspiring, and uplifting, rather than focusing on negative or triggering content.

Another important strategy is to cultivate a sense of gratitude and appreciation for the blessings in our own lives, rather than focusing on what we lack or what others have. This can involve practicing daily gratitude exercises, such as writing down three things we are grateful for each day or taking time to reflect on the good things in our lives.

Ultimately, the key to contentment is not about having more, achieving more, or comparing ourselves to others. It's about finding meaning, purpose, and joy in our own lives, regardless of our circumstances or external factors. By using social media in a mindful and intentional way, and focusing on gratitude and appreciation for what we have, we can unlock the power of contentment and achieve lasting happiness and fulfillment.

26: Finding Balance: The Importance of Work-Life Balance for Contentment

Introduction

In today's fast-paced world, it can be challenging to achieve a sense of balance between work and life. With the advent of technology and the internet, work has become more accessible than ever before, leading to longer working hours and blurring the lines between work and personal time. However, finding a balance between work and life is crucial for achieving contentment and lasting happiness. In this chapter, we will explore the importance of work-life balance and how it can be achieved.

Defining Work-Life Balance

Work-life balance refers to the equilibrium between work and personal life. It involves managing one's time, energy, and resources in a way that allows them to meet their professional obligations while also maintaining a healthy personal life. Achieving work-life balance means giving equal attention to work and personal life, without one area overpowering the other.

26: FINDING BALANCE: THE IMPORTANCE OF WORK-LIFE BALANCE FOR CONTENTMENT

Importance of Work-Life Balance for Contentment

Achieving work-life balance is essential for several reasons, including:

Reduced Stress and Burnout: An imbalance between work and personal life can lead to stress and burnout. When work takes over your life, it can lead to exhaustion, decreased productivity, and even physical and mental health issues. On the other hand, having enough time for personal activities and relationships can reduce stress levels and prevent burnout.

Improved Health: Finding a balance between work and life can also lead to improved health. Physical activities such as exercise, social activities, and hobbies can help to reduce stress, improve mood, and prevent diseases such as obesity, heart disease, and depression.

Better Relationships: Spending quality time with family and friends can strengthen relationships and lead to better mental health. Personal relationships are an essential part of life, and neglecting them can lead to feelings of loneliness and isolation.

26: FINDING BALANCE: THE IMPORTANCE OF WORK-LIFE BALANCE FOR CONTENTMENT

Increased Productivity: Finding a balance between work and personal life can also lead to increased productivity. When you have enough time for personal activities and hobbies, you can return to work feeling refreshed, motivated, and energized. Additionally, by prioritizing tasks and managing your time more effectively, you can accomplish more in less time.

Strategies for Achieving Work-Life Balance

Set Boundaries: One of the most important strategies for achieving work-life balance is setting boundaries. This includes setting limits on work hours, prioritizing personal time, and communicating your needs to your employer or colleagues. For example, if you are consistently working overtime, speak to your employer about the need for a better work-life balance.

Prioritize Personal Time: Another important strategy is to prioritize personal time. This includes making time for hobbies, exercise, social activities, and self-care. By prioritizing personal time, you can reduce stress levels, improve your mental health, and prevent burnout.

26: FINDING BALANCE: THE IMPORTANCE OF WORK-LIFE BALANCE FOR CONTENTMENT

Manage Your Time Effectively: Managing your time effectively is also crucial for achieving work-life balance. This involves prioritizing tasks, avoiding distractions, and being mindful of your time. Use a calendar or planner to schedule your day, and set realistic deadlines for tasks.

Practice Self-Care: Practicing self-care is an essential part of achieving work-life balance. This includes getting enough sleep, eating a healthy diet, and engaging in activities that promote relaxation and stress reduction, such as meditation, yoga, or reading.

Seek Support: Seeking support from family, friends, or a therapist can also be helpful in achieving work-life balance. Talking to someone can provide perspective, support, and encouragement, helping you to stay motivated and focused on your goals.

Inspiring Stories of Achieving Work-Life Balance

Many people have successfully achieved work-life balance, despite the challenges of today's fast-paced world. For example, Mary, a mother of three, struggled to balance her job as a nurse with her family obligations. However, by setting boundaries, prioritizing personal time, and seeking support from her partner and friends, Mary was able to achieve a sense of balance. She started scheduling regular family outings and making time for hobbies like gardening, which helped her reduce stress levels and improve her overall well-being.

Similarly, Tom, a software developer, struggled with burnout and exhaustion due to long working hours and high-pressure deadlines. However, by implementing time management strategies, prioritizing exercise and self-care, and setting boundaries on his work hours, Tom was able to achieve a better work-life balance. He found that taking breaks and engaging in physical activities like hiking helped him stay focused and energized at work.

Practical Tools for Achieving Work-Life Balance

There are several practical tools that can help you achieve work-life balance. These include:

Time Management Apps: There are several time management apps available that can help you prioritize tasks, manage your schedule, and avoid distractions. These include apps like Trello, Asana, and RescueTime.

Fitness Trackers: Fitness trackers can help you monitor your physical activity levels and track your progress towards fitness goals. This can be a great way to incorporate exercise into your daily routine and reduce stress levels.

Mindfulness Apps: Mindfulness apps like Headspace and Calm can help you practice mindfulness and relaxation techniques, reducing stress levels and promoting a sense of well-being.

Online Courses: There are several online courses available that can help you develop skills in time management, stress reduction, and work-life balance. These can be a great way to learn new strategies and techniques for achieving balance in your life.

Conclusion

Achieving work-life balance is crucial for contentment and lasting happiness. It involves managing one's time, energy, and resources in a way that allows them to meet their professional obligations while also maintaining a healthy personal life. By setting boundaries, prioritizing personal time, managing your time effectively, practicing self-care, and seeking support, you can achieve a sense of balance in your life. Remember, finding balance is not a one-time event but a continual process that requires ongoing attention and effort.

27: The Connection between Finances and Contentment: The Role of Money in Happiness

Money is often considered one of the most important factors in achieving happiness. Many people believe that having more money will automatically lead to greater contentment in life. However, research has shown that while money can certainly contribute to happiness, it is not the only or even the most important factor.

In this chapter, we will explore the relationship between finances and contentment. We will examine the ways in which money can impact our happiness, and we will discuss some of the strategies and tools that can help us achieve financial security and contentment.

The Importance of Financial Security

One of the most significant ways in which finances can impact our contentment is through financial security. When we feel financially secure, we have a sense of stability and peace of mind. We are less likely to worry about how we will pay our bills or meet our basic needs, and we can focus more on pursuing our goals and enjoying life.

27: THE CONNECTION BETWEEN FINANCES AND CONTENTMENT: THE ROLE OF MONEY IN HAPPINESS

On the other hand, when we are struggling financially, it can be challenging to feel content. We may feel stressed, anxious, and overwhelmed by the constant pressure to make ends meet. We may have to make difficult choices about how to spend our money, and we may feel like we are always one unexpected expense away from financial disaster.

Financial security is not just about having a lot of money; it is about having enough to cover our basic needs and feel comfortable. This can vary depending on our circumstances, but it typically includes things like housing, food, transportation, and healthcare. When we have these things covered, we are more likely to feel content and satisfied with our lives.

The Connection between Money and Happiness

While financial security is essential for contentment, having more money beyond our basic needs does not necessarily equate to greater happiness. Research has shown that once our basic needs are met, the relationship between money and happiness is much more complex.

27: THE CONNECTION BETWEEN FINANCES AND CONTENTMENT: THE ROLE OF MONEY IN HAPPINESS

One reason for this is that our brains are wired to adapt to our circumstances. This means that we quickly get used to having more money and the things that money can buy. The initial thrill of buying a new car or taking a fancy vacation fades over time, and we are left with a sense of normalcy. This is known as the hedonic treadmill, and it means that we need more and more money to achieve the same level of happiness.

Another reason why money does not always lead to happiness is that it can be a double-edged sword. While money can buy us things that bring us joy and comfort, it can also create stress and anxiety. For example, people who are wealthy may feel pressure to maintain their lifestyle or keep up with their peers. They may worry about losing their money or being taken advantage of by others.

Additionally, research has shown that the way we spend our money can have a significant impact on our happiness. Spending money on experiences, such as travel or concerts, tends to bring more joy than spending money on material possessions. This is because experiences create lasting memories and connections with others, while material possessions often lose their appeal over time.

Strategies for Achieving Financial Contentment

Given the complex relationship between money and happiness, it can be challenging to know how to achieve financial contentment. However, there are several strategies and tools that can help.

First and foremost, it is essential to prioritize financial security. This means creating a budget, living within our means, and building an emergency fund. It also means investing in our education and career development to increase our earning potential over time.

Beyond financial security, it is also important to be intentional about how we spend our money. This means focusing on experiences rather than material possessions and being mindful of our purchases. We can also find ways to give back to our communities and support causes that are meaningful to us, which can bring a sense of purpose and fulfillment.

Another strategy for achieving financial contentment is to

cultivate gratitude and contentment in our lives. This means recognizing and appreciating what we have rather than always striving for more. It means practicing gratitude for the small things in life, such as a beautiful sunset or a kind gesture from a friend.

In addition to these strategies, there are several practical tools that can help us achieve financial contentment. These include:

Setting financial goals: By setting clear financial goals, we can create a roadmap for achieving financial security and contentment. This might include saving for a down payment on a house, paying off debt, or investing for retirement.

Automating our finances: By automating our savings and bills, we can take the stress out of managing our money. This can help us stay on track with our financial goals and reduce the risk of overspending.

Seeking professional advice: Financial advisors and planners can provide valuable guidance on investing, saving, and managing our money. They can help us create a customized financial plan that aligns with our goals and values.

Practicing mindfulness: Mindfulness practices, such as meditation and yoga, can help us cultivate a greater sense of awareness and contentment in our lives. By being more present in the moment, we can reduce stress and anxiety around our finances and feel more content with what we have.

Conclusion

In conclusion, the relationship between finances and contentment is complex and multi-faceted. While financial security is important for our well-being, having more money does not necessarily equate to greater happiness. Instead, achieving financial contentment requires a combination of strategies and tools, including prioritizing financial security, being intentional about how we spend our money, and cultivating gratitude and mindfulness in our lives.

By taking a holistic approach to our finances and prioritizing our well-being over our material possessions, we can unlock the power of contentment and achieve lasting happiness in our lives.

28: Overcoming Materialism: Finding Contentment Beyond Consumerism

Introduction

Materialism is a common trait in today's society, where people are constantly encouraged to acquire more, to spend more, and to consume more. The idea that owning more things will make us happier is deeply ingrained in our culture. However, research shows that material possessions only bring temporary happiness and that there are better ways to find contentment in life. This chapter will explore the negative effects of materialism, the benefits of living a simpler life, and how to overcome the pull of consumerism.

The Negative Effects of Materialism

The pursuit of material possessions can have a negative impact on our well-being. Studies have shown that people who place a high value on material possessions are more likely to experience negative emotions such as anxiety, depression, and stress. They are also more likely to have a lower sense of self-esteem and to experience lower levels of life satisfaction.

28: OVERCOMING MATERIALISM: FINDING CONTENTMENT BEYOND CONSUMERISM

One reason for this is that material possessions are often linked to social status. We may feel that we need to have certain things in order to fit in with our peers or to signal our success to others. This can create a cycle of wanting more and more, as we try to keep up with others or to maintain a certain image.

Another reason why materialism can be detrimental to our well-being is that it can lead to a focus on external factors rather than internal ones. We may believe that our happiness is dependent on what we own or how much money we make, rather than on our relationships, our health, or our personal growth. This can lead to a sense of emptiness or lack of purpose, as we realize that material possessions do not bring us the lasting fulfillment we crave.

The Benefits of Living a Simpler Life

Living a simpler life can have numerous benefits for our well-being. By reducing our focus on material possessions and consumerism, we can free up our time and energy to focus on other areas of life that are more fulfilling. Some benefits of living a simpler life include:

28: OVERCOMING MATERIALISM: FINDING CONTENTMENT BEYOND CONSUMERISM

Greater contentment: By focusing on what we already have and finding joy in the simple things, we can experience greater contentment and satisfaction in life.

Reduced stress: When we are not constantly chasing after the next thing to buy, we can experience a sense of calm and reduced stress.

Improved relationships: By valuing relationships over possessions, we can deepen our connections with others and experience greater intimacy and support.

Increased creativity: By being more mindful and present in our daily lives, we can tap into our creativity and find new ways to express ourselves.

Improved health: By reducing our exposure to consumer culture and the stress that comes with it, we can improve our physical and mental health.

How to Overcome Materialism

Overcoming materialism is not always easy, but it is possible with the right strategies and mindset. Here are some tips for finding contentment beyond consumerism:

28: OVERCOMING MATERIALISM: FINDING CONTENT-MENT BEYOND CONSUMERISM

Practice gratitude: By focusing on what we already have and expressing gratitude for it, we can shift our mindset away from constantly wanting more.

Simplify your life: Look for ways to simplify your life, such as decluttering your home or reducing your commitments. This can free up time and energy to focus on what is truly important.

Connect with others: Invest in your relationships with others, whether that means spending more time with loved ones or volunteering in your community. By valuing relationships over possessions, we can find greater fulfillment and purpose in life.

Focus on experiences: Instead of buying things, focus on experiences that bring you joy, such as travel, hobbies, or spending time in nature. These experiences can create lasting memories and deepen your sense of contentment.

Practice mindfulness: By being more mindful and present in your daily life, you can become more aware of your own thoughts and feelings, and learn to appreciate the present moment. This can help you avoid getting caught up in the cycle of wanting more, and instead find contentment in the present.

Challenge societal norms: Recognize that the constant push to consume more is not a natural or inevitable part of life, but rather a product of societal norms and pressures. Challenge these norms by questioning the messages you receive from media and advertising, and making conscious choices about what you buy and why.

Set realistic goals: Instead of setting goals based on acquiring more possessions, focus on goals that are meaningful and fulfilling in their own right, such as learning a new skill, building a strong relationship, or making a positive impact in your community.

Practice self-compassion: Recognize that overcoming materialism is a journey, and that it's okay to slip up or struggle along the way. Practice self-compassion by being kind to yourself and focusing on progress rather than perfection.

Conclusion

28: OVERCOMING MATERIALISM: FINDING CONTENT-MENT BEYOND CONSUMERISM

In conclusion, materialism can have a negative impact on our well-being, but it is possible to find contentment beyond consumerism. By focusing on what is truly important in life, such as relationships, experiences, and personal growth, we can find lasting fulfillment and happiness. By practicing gratitude, simplifying our lives, connecting with others, focusing on experiences, practicing mindfulness, challenging societal norms, setting realistic goals, and practicing self-compassion, we can overcome the pull of materialism and unlock the power of contentment.

29: The Power of Giving: The Joy of Generosity and Compassion

In this chapter, we will explore the power of giving and the joy of generosity and compassion. Giving is one of the most powerful things we can do to bring happiness and fulfillment into our lives. It is an act of kindness that not only benefits the person who receives, but also the person who gives. Giving can be in the form of time, money, or resources, and it can be done in countless ways.

Giving is an expression of love and compassion that is fundamental to our humanity. It is an act that brings us closer to one another, and it helps us to connect with the world around us. Giving is a way to show gratitude for what we have and to share our blessings with others.

One of the reasons that giving is so powerful is that it has a ripple effect. When we give to others, we inspire them to give to others as well. This creates a cycle of generosity that spreads throughout our communities, making them stronger and more compassionate. When we give, we also create a sense of abundance in our lives, which can help us to feel more content and fulfilled.

29: THE POWER OF GIVING: THE JOY OF GENEROSITY AND COMPASSION

Giving doesn't have to be a grand gesture to be meaningful. Small acts of kindness can have a profound impact on the people around us. A simple smile or a kind word can brighten someone's day and remind them that they are not alone. Giving can also be done anonymously, which can make the act even more meaningful. Anonymous giving allows us to give without expecting anything in return, which can be a powerful way to express our compassion and generosity.

There are many benefits to giving. When we give, we experience a sense of satisfaction and fulfillment that comes from knowing that we have made a difference in someone's life. Giving can also help us to feel more connected to others, which can improve our sense of well-being and reduce feelings of loneliness and isolation. Giving can also help us to develop a sense of purpose and meaning in our lives, which can lead to greater contentment and happiness.

Giving can also have physical health benefits. Studies have shown that people who give to others are less likely to experience chronic stress, depression, and anxiety. Giving can also improve our immune system function and reduce inflammation, which can help to protect us against a range of diseases.

One of the keys to giving is to do it in a way that is authentic and meaningful to us. We should give in a way that feels natural and aligned with our values and beliefs. For some people, this might mean volunteering at a local charity, while for others it might mean donating money or resources to a cause they care about. Whatever form our giving takes, it should be something that brings us joy and a sense of purpose.

It is also important to remember that giving is not always easy. Sometimes it can be challenging to find the time, energy, or resources to give to others. However, when we push through these challenges and make the effort to give, we often find that the rewards are worth it. Giving can help us to develop greater empathy and compassion, which can lead to greater understanding and connection with the people around us.

In conclusion, the power of giving is a force that can transform our lives and the lives of those around us. By giving of ourselves, we can experience a sense of purpose, fulfillment, and joy that is unparalleled. Whether we give our time, money, or resources, we can make a difference in the world and leave a positive impact on the people we encounter. Let us embrace the joy of generosity and compassion and discover the transformative power of giving.

30: Embracing Diversity: The Role of Acceptance and Tolerance in Contentment

Contentment is often considered as the ultimate goal of life. We all want to achieve it but the path towards contentment is not an easy one. It requires a lot of effort, patience, and understanding of oneself and others. In this chapter, we will explore the importance of embracing diversity and how acceptance and tolerance can help us achieve contentment in life.

Diversity is all around us. It comes in many forms, such as race, ethnicity, gender, sexuality, religion, and many more. Each individual is unique and has their own set of beliefs, values, and experiences that shape their identity. Embracing diversity means accepting and respecting these differences and recognizing the value they bring to our lives.

However, the reality is that not everyone embraces diversity. Prejudice, discrimination, and intolerance still exist in many parts of the world. These negative attitudes can create division, conflict, and misery in our lives. In order to achieve contentment, it is important to recognize and address these issues.

One way to embrace diversity is through acceptance. Acceptance means acknowledging and embracing the differences in others without judgment or criticism. It requires an open mind and a willingness to learn about other cultures, beliefs, and experiences. Acceptance also means recognizing our own biases and working to overcome them.

Tolerance is another important aspect of embracing diversity. Tolerance means respecting the differences in others, even if we do not agree with or understand them. It requires empathy and compassion towards those who are different from us. Tolerance also means standing up against discrimination and prejudice in all its forms.

The benefits of embracing diversity are numerous. It creates a sense of unity and harmony in our communities. It allows us to learn from others and broaden our perspectives. It also promotes empathy and understanding, which can lead to more meaningful relationships and a deeper appreciation for the world around us.

However, embracing diversity is not always easy. It requires

us to step out of our comfort zones and confront our own biases and prejudices. It may also require us to challenge the
negative attitudes and beliefs of those around us. This can
be a difficult and uncomfortable process, but it is necessary
if we want to achieve contentment in our lives.

There are several strategies that can help us embrace diversity and cultivate acceptance and tolerance. One strategy
is to educate ourselves about different cultures, religions,
and experiences. This can be done through reading books,
watching documentaries, or attending cultural events. By
learning about other people's experiences, we can gain a
better understanding of their perspectives and develop empathy towards them.

Another strategy is to practice active listening. Active listening means paying attention to what someone is saying
without interrupting or judging them. It involves asking
questions and seeking clarification to ensure that we understand the other person's perspective. By practicing active
listening, we can build stronger relationships and promote
understanding and acceptance.

It is also important to be mindful of our own biases and prejudices. We all have them, but it is up to us to recognize and address them. This may involve reflecting on our own experiences and beliefs and examining how they may have shaped our attitudes towards others. It may also involve seeking feedback from others and being open to constructive criticism.

In conclusion, embracing diversity is essential for achieving contentment in life. Acceptance and tolerance are the key to embracing diversity and promoting unity and understanding in our communities. By educating ourselves, practicing active listening, and being mindful of our own biases and prejudices, we can cultivate acceptance and tolerance and create a more fulfilling and meaningful life for ourselves and those around us.

31: Finding Community: The Importance of Connection and Belonging

As human beings, we are social creatures. We have a deep need to connect with others and to feel a sense of belonging. This need for community is hard-wired into our DNA, and it plays a vital role in our mental, emotional, and even physical well-being. In this chapter, we will explore the importance of connection and belonging and how we can cultivate these essential elements in our lives.

The Power of Connection

Connection is the glue that holds us together. It is the foundation of all human relationships, and it is essential for our well-being. When we feel connected to others, we feel seen, heard, and understood. We feel like we belong, and we know that we are not alone.

Connection is crucial for our mental health. Studies have shown that people who have strong social connections are less likely to suffer from depression, anxiety, and other mental health issues. They are also more resilient in the face of stress and adversity.

Connection is also vital for our physical health. Research has found that people who have strong social connections live longer and have better overall health than those who are socially isolated. Social connection can even help to boost our immune system, lower our blood pressure, and reduce our risk of chronic diseases.

The Importance of Belonging

Belonging is the feeling that we are part of something larger than ourselves. It is the sense of being connected to a group or community that shares our values, interests, and experiences. When we feel like we belong, we feel accepted, supported, and valued.

Belonging is crucial for our self-esteem. When we feel like we belong, we feel like we are worthy of love and acceptance. We know that we have something to offer, and we feel more confident in ourselves.

Belonging is also important for our sense of purpose. When we feel like we belong to a group or community, we have a sense of shared mission or vision. We know that we are working towards something greater than ourselves, and this can give us a sense of meaning and direction in our lives.

The Challenges of Finding Community

Despite the many benefits of connection and belonging, finding community can be challenging. In our fast-paced, modern world, we are often disconnected from our neighbors, colleagues, and even our own families. We may feel isolated, lonely, or misunderstood, even when we are surrounded by people.

Finding community can also be challenging because we all have unique needs and preferences. What works for one person may not work for another. Some people prefer to connect with others online, while others prefer face-to-face interactions. Some people thrive in large, bustling communities, while others prefer small, intimate groups.

Despite these challenges, finding community is possible. It may take some time, effort, and patience, but it is worth it for the many benefits that come with connection and belonging.

Strategies for Finding Community

31: FINDING COMMUNITY: THE IMPORTANCE OF CONNECTION AND BELONGING

There are many strategies for finding community, and the key is to find what works best for you. Here are some ideas to get you started:

Volunteer: Volunteering is a great way to connect with others who share your values and interests. You can find volunteer opportunities through local organizations, online platforms, or social media.

Join a club or organization: Whether you are interested in sports, arts, or hobbies, there is likely a club or organization in your area that caters to your interests. Joining a group can help you meet like-minded people and build lasting relationships.

Attend events: From community festivals to networking events, there are many opportunities to connect with others in your area. Attend events that interest you, and be open to meeting new people.

Take a class: Whether you are interested in learning a new skill or simply want to meet new people, taking a class can be a great way to connect with others. Look for classes in your area that cater to your interests, such as cooking, dancing, or photography.

Join online communities: In addition to offline communities, there are many online communities where you can connect with others who share your interests. From Facebook groups to online forums, there are many options to choose from.

Attend religious services: If you are religious or spiritual, attending services at your local place of worship can be a great way to connect with others who share your beliefs.

Participate in sports or fitness activities: Whether you enjoy running, hiking, or playing team sports, there are many opportunities to connect with others through physical activities.

Meetup groups: Meetup is a website that allows you to find groups of people who share your interests and hobbies. You can join groups in your area and attend events that cater to your interests.

Building and Maintaining Relationships

Once you have found a community or group of people that

you connect with, it is important to build and maintain relationships. Here are some tips for doing so:

Be consistent: Show up regularly to events and activities, and make an effort to get to know people.

Be authentic: Be yourself, and don't be afraid to share your interests, thoughts, and feelings with others.

Listen actively: When you are talking with others, make an effort to listen actively and show interest in what they have to say.

Be supportive: Offer support and encouragement to others, and be willing to help out when needed.

Practice forgiveness: No one is perfect, and conflicts are bound to arise in any relationship. Practice forgiveness and let go of grudges to maintain healthy relationships.

Stay in touch: Keep in touch with people through social media, email, or phone calls. Make an effort to stay connected, even when you can't see each other in person.

The Benefits of Community

31: FINDING COMMUNITY: THE IMPORTANCE OF CONNECTION AND BELONGING

When we find a community or group of people that we connect with, the benefits can be profound. Here are some of the many benefits of community:

– Increased sense of belonging and connection

– Improved mental health and well-being

– Increased self-esteem and confidence

– Greater sense of purpose and meaning in life

– Opportunities for personal growth and learning

– Enhanced social support and resilience in times of stress

– Improved physical health and longevity

Conclusion

Finding community is an essential part of cultivating contentment and happiness in our lives. Connection and belonging are crucial for our mental, emotional, and physical well-being, and they can help us to find purpose, meaning, and direction in our lives. While finding community may be challenging, there are many strategies that can help us to

connect with others and build lasting relationships. By prioritizing connection and belonging in our lives, we can unlock the power of contentment and achieve lasting happiness.

32: The Role of Creativity: Nurturing Your Creative Side for Contentment

Introduction

Humans are inherently creative beings. We are constantly creating, whether it's through art, music, writing, or even problem-solving. However, as we grow older, many of us lose touch with our creative side. We become too busy with work, family, and other responsibilities to nurture our artistic inclinations. Yet, creativity is essential to living a fulfilling life. In this chapter, we'll explore the role of creativity in contentment and how you can nurture your creative side to achieve lasting happiness.

The Link between Creativity and Contentment

Creativity is often associated with happiness and contentment. In fact, studies have shown that engaging in creative activities can have a positive impact on mental health and well-being. This is because creativity allows us to express ourselves, tap into our emotions, and explore new ideas and perspectives.

32: THE ROLE OF CREATIVITY: NURTURING YOUR CREATIVE SIDE FOR CONTENTMENT

Furthermore, being creative can give us a sense of purpose and meaning. When we create something, whether it's a painting, a song, or a poem, we are putting a part of ourselves into the world. This can be incredibly fulfilling and can help us feel like we are contributing something valuable.

In addition, engaging in creative activities can also help us feel more present and mindful. When we're in the zone, completely focused on our creative work, we're not thinking about the past or the future. We're simply immersed in the present moment, which can be incredibly grounding and calming.

Nurturing Your Creative Side

Now that we've established the link between creativity and contentment, let's explore how you can nurture your creative side.

Make time for creative activities

The first step to nurturing your creative side is to make time for creative activities. This might mean carving out time in your schedule each week for painting, writing, or playing music. It could also mean incorporating creativity into your daily routine, such as by doodling in a sketchbook during your lunch break or writing a poem before bed.

Try something new

Another way to nurture your creative side is to try something new. If you've always been a writer, why not try painting? If you've never played an instrument before, why not take up guitar lessons? Trying new creative pursuits can help you break out of your comfort zone and discover new talents and passions.

Embrace imperfection

One of the biggest barriers to creativity is the fear of failure or not being good enough. However, it's important to remember that creativity is not about being perfect. It's about expressing yourself and exploring new ideas. Embrace imperfection and allow yourself to make mistakes. This will free you up to take risks and try new things.

Surround yourself with inspiration

32: THE ROLE OF CREATIVITY: NURTURING YOUR CREATIVE SIDE FOR CONTENTMENT

Another way to nurture your creative side is to surround yourself with inspiration. This might mean setting up a dedicated space for your creative work, filled with art supplies, books, and music. It could also mean surrounding yourself with people who inspire you, such as other artists or writers.

Practice self-care

Finally, it's important to practice self-care when nurturing your creative side. Creativity can be a powerful tool for self-expression and healing, but it can also be draining. Make sure you're taking care of your physical and mental health by getting enough sleep, eating well, and taking breaks when you need them.

Conclusion

In conclusion, creativity is an essential part of living a fulfilling life. It allows us to express ourselves, explore new ideas, and find meaning and purpose. By nurturing your creative side, you can tap into the power of creativity and unlock the secrets to lasting happiness and contentment. So go ahead, pick up that paintbrush or guitar and let your creativity flow!

33: Embracing Change: Finding Contentment in Transitions and New Beginnings

Change is a fundamental aspect of life. As the old adage goes, the only constant in life is change. We experience changes in our personal lives, our relationships, our careers, and even in the world around us. Some changes are small and manageable, while others are more significant and can be overwhelming. Nevertheless, change is an essential ingredient for growth and progress.

For many people, change can be a source of anxiety and fear. It's natural to feel comfortable in the familiar and the predictable. However, as we navigate through life, we will inevitably encounter situations that challenge us to step out of our comfort zone and embrace new opportunities. This can be a difficult and uncomfortable process, but it's also an essential part of personal and professional development.

In this chapter, we'll explore the topic of embracing change and finding contentment in transitions and new beginnings. We'll look at the psychology behind change, why it can be so challenging, and how we can develop the resilience and adaptability to navigate through these transitions successfully. We'll also examine some practical strategies for embracing change, managing stress, and finding contentment in new beginnings.

Understanding the Psychology of Change

To understand why change can be so challenging, it's helpful to examine the psychology behind our reactions to change. The human brain is wired to seek safety and stability, and any threat to that stability can trigger a stress response. When we're faced with a significant change, our brains perceive it as a potential threat, and we experience a range of emotions, including fear, anxiety, and uncertainty.

These emotional responses are entirely normal, but they can also be overwhelming and paralyzing. We may find ourselves stuck in a state of indecision or avoidance, unable to move forward. However, it's important to remember that change is not inherently negative. In fact, change can be a catalyst for growth and transformation. It's all about how we choose to approach it.

Developing Resilience and Adaptability

33: EMBRACING CHANGE: FINDING CONTENTMENT IN TRANSITIONS AND NEW BEGINNINGS

One of the keys to embracing change is developing resilience and adaptability. Resilience is the ability to bounce back from adversity and overcome challenges. Adaptability is the capacity to adjust to new situations and environments. Together, these traits form a powerful combination that can help us navigate through transitions and find contentment in new beginnings.

So how do we develop resilience and adaptability? There are several strategies that can help:

Practice Mindfulness - Mindfulness is the practice of being present and fully engaged in the current moment. It can help us develop a sense of calm and perspective, which can be especially helpful during times of change and transition.

Build a Support Network - Having a strong support network of friends, family, and colleagues can provide a sense of security and comfort during times of change. Reach out to others for support and encouragement.

Cultivate a Growth Mindset - A growth mindset is the belief that our abilities and intelligence can be developed over time. When we approach challenges with a growth mindset, we are more likely to persevere and overcome obstacles.

Focus on What You Can Control - Change can often feel overwhelming because there are so many variables outside of our control. Instead of fixating on these external factors, focus on what you can control - your attitude, your actions, and your perspective.

Practical Strategies for Embracing Change

In addition to developing resilience and adaptability, there are several practical strategies that can help us embrace change and find contentment in new beginnings.

Set Realistic Expectations - Change can be a slow and gradual process, so it's essential to set realistic expectations for yourself. Don't expect to feel comfortable and settled in a new situation overnight. Give yourself time to adjust and acclimate.

Take Small Steps - Change can be overwhelming when we try to tackle it all at once. Instead, break the process down into small, manageable steps. Focus on making one small change at a time, and celebrate each step of progress along the way.

Practice Self-Care - During times of change and transition, it's essential to take care of yourself both physically and emotionally. Make sure you're getting enough rest, eating well, and engaging in activities that bring you joy and relaxation.

Stay Flexible - Change can be unpredictable, and things may not always go as planned. Stay flexible and be willing to adjust your plans and expectations as needed.

Embrace the Unknown - Change often involves stepping into the unknown, and that can be scary. However, it can also be exciting and full of potential. Embrace the uncertainty and focus on the possibilities that lie ahead.

Finding Contentment in New Beginnings

Finally, it's important to remember that contentment is possible even in the midst of change and transition. Contentment is not about having everything figured out or achieving a state of perfection. Instead, contentment is about finding peace and joy in the present moment, no matter what circumstances we may be facing.

To find contentment in new beginnings, it can be helpful to focus on the positive aspects of the change. Look for the opportunities and potential that lie ahead, and focus on the things that you're grateful for in your current situation. Practice gratitude and mindfulness, and take time to reflect on your values and priorities.

In conclusion, change is an essential aspect of life, and it's something that we will all encounter at various points in our journey. While change can be challenging, it's also an opportunity for growth and transformation. By developing resilience and adaptability, practicing practical strategies for embracing change, and focusing on finding contentment in new beginnings, we can navigate through transitions with greater ease and joy.

34: The Benefits of Travel: Exploring New Places for Contentment

Introduction

Many people believe that traveling is an excellent way to find contentment and happiness. It allows you to escape your daily routine, experience new cultures, and explore different parts of the world. Traveling can provide an opportunity for personal growth and can offer many benefits for your mental, emotional, and physical health. In this chapter, we will explore the benefits of travel and how it can help you achieve contentment.

Increased Self-Awareness

Traveling to new places can provide you with a unique opportunity for self-discovery. It allows you to step outside of your comfort zone and challenge yourself to try new things. You may find yourself in situations that you never thought possible, which can help you learn more about your strengths and weaknesses.

When you travel, you also have the chance to reflect on your life and gain perspective. Being away from your daily routine can help you reevaluate your priorities and make necessary changes. You may also gain a better understanding of your values, beliefs, and purpose in life. All of these insights can contribute to a greater sense of self-awareness and contentment.

Improved Mental Health

Traveling can also have a positive impact on your mental health. It can reduce stress, anxiety, and depression by providing you with a break from your daily responsibilities. When you travel, you have the chance to disconnect from technology and connect with nature and your surroundings. This can help you feel more present and mindful, which can contribute to a greater sense of calm and contentment.

Traveling can also provide you with a sense of adventure and excitement. Trying new things and exploring unfamiliar places can help you feel more alive and engaged in the world. This can lead to a greater sense of joy and fulfillment, which can improve your overall mental health and well-being.

Enhanced Creativity

34: THE BENEFITS OF TRAVEL: EXPLORING NEW PLACES FOR CONTENTMENT

Traveling can also stimulate your creativity and imagination. When you visit new places, you are exposed to different cultures, people, and ways of life. This can inspire new ideas and perspectives, which can contribute to greater creativity.

You may also find that traveling helps you break free from creative blocks or mental ruts. Being in a new environment can help you think differently and approach problems in new ways. This can be particularly beneficial for artists, writers, and other creatives who need to tap into their imaginations to produce their best work.

Greater Empathy and Understanding

Traveling to new places can also help you develop greater empathy and understanding for others. When you are exposed to different cultures and ways of life, you can gain a deeper appreciation for diversity and the richness of the human experience. This can help you become more tolerant, open-minded, and accepting of others, which can contribute to greater contentment and peace of mind.

When you travel, you also have the opportunity to connect

with people from different backgrounds and perspectives. This can help you develop greater empathy and compassion for others, which can be beneficial for both your personal and professional relationships.

Practical Benefits

In addition to the mental, emotional, and creative benefits of travel, there are also practical benefits to exploring new places. Traveling can help you develop new skills, such as language proficiency or navigation skills. It can also provide you with opportunities to network, learn from others, and gain new career insights.

Traveling can also be a great way to disconnect from technology and recharge your batteries. It allows you to take a break from the stresses of work and responsibilities and focus on self-care and rejuvenation. This can contribute to greater overall health and wellbeing, which can help you achieve greater contentment and happiness.

Conclusion

Traveling is an excellent way to find contentment and happiness. It provides many benefits for your mental, emotional, and physical health, as well as practical benefits for your personal and professional life. By exploring new places and experiencing different cultures, you can gain a greater sense of self-awareness, improve your mental health, enhance your creativity, and develop greater empathy and understanding for others.

Whether you travel solo or with friends and family, it's important to approach each trip with an open mind and a willingness to learn and grow. Take the time to immerse yourself in new experiences, try new foods, and connect with locals. Embrace the challenges and opportunities that come with travel, and allow yourself to be transformed by the experience.

In addition to the benefits of travel, it's also important to consider the environmental and social impacts of tourism. When traveling, it's important to be mindful of your impact on local communities and the environment. Consider supporting sustainable tourism initiatives and responsible travel practices to ensure that your travels have a positive impact on the world around you.

34: THE BENEFITS OF TRAVEL: EXPLORING NEW PLACES FOR CONTENTMENT

In conclusion, traveling is a powerful tool for finding contentment and happiness. It can provide you with unique opportunities for personal growth and can contribute to greater overall health and wellbeing. By exploring new places and experiencing different cultures, you can gain a deeper appreciation for the world around you and develop a greater sense of contentment and peace of mind. So pack your bags, hit the road, and discover the transformative power of travel for yourself.

35: Pursuing Lifelong Learning: The Importance of Growth and Development for Contentment

Contentment is not just about being satisfied with what you have, but also about continuous growth and development. Pursuing lifelong learning is a crucial aspect of achieving contentment. It is not limited to formal education or training but encompasses all forms of personal growth and development.

The pursuit of lifelong learning allows individuals to broaden their knowledge, skills, and perspectives. It enables them to gain a deeper understanding of themselves, others, and the world around them. Through lifelong learning, individuals can explore their interests, passions, and values, and discover new ones. It can open up new opportunities and help individuals achieve their goals and aspirations.

The benefits of lifelong learning are numerous. It can enhance cognitive function, improve memory, and delay the onset of cognitive decline. It can also improve mental health by reducing stress, anxiety, and depression. Lifelong learning can lead to personal and professional growth, enhance job performance, and increase earning potential. Moreover, it can foster social connections, promote community involvement, and contribute to personal fulfillment.

There are various ways to pursue lifelong learning, depending on one's interests, learning style, and preferences. Formal education is one way to pursue lifelong learning, whether it be through traditional academic institutions or online courses. Informal learning opportunities are also available, such as reading books, attending seminars, workshops, or conferences, participating in online communities, or engaging in self-directed learning.

One effective way to pursue lifelong learning is by setting learning goals. This involves identifying areas of interest or skill development and setting specific, measurable, achievable, relevant, and time-bound (SMART) goals. For instance, one may set a goal to learn a new language, develop a new skill, or deepen their knowledge of a particular subject. By setting goals, individuals can focus their efforts and track their progress, which can enhance motivation and commitment.

35: PURSUING LIFELONG LEARNING: THE IMPORTANCE OF GROWTH AND DEVELOPMENT FOR CONTENTMENT

Another crucial aspect of pursuing lifelong learning is adopting a growth mindset. A growth mindset is a belief that abilities and intelligence can be developed through hard work, dedication, and perseverance. It is a mindset that embraces challenges, values effort and persistence, and sees failure as an opportunity for learning and growth. By adopting a growth mindset, individuals can overcome self-limiting beliefs, take risks, and embrace new challenges, which can lead to personal and professional growth.

In addition to setting goals and adopting a growth mindset, seeking feedback is another essential aspect of pursuing lifelong learning. Feedback provides individuals with valuable information on their strengths, weaknesses, and areas for improvement. It can help individuals identify blind spots, overcome obstacles, and achieve their goals more effectively. Moreover, feedback can foster self-awareness, promote self-reflection, and enhance personal growth and development.

Finally, building a learning community is crucial for pursuing lifelong learning. Learning communities are groups of individuals who share common interests, goals, and values and support each other in their learning journeys. Learning communities can provide individuals with opportunities for collaboration, feedback, and mentorship. They can also offer a sense of belonging, connection, and support, which can enhance motivation and commitment to learning.

In conclusion, pursuing lifelong learning is a crucial aspect of achieving contentment. It allows individuals to broaden their knowledge, skills, and perspectives, and enhance personal and professional growth. By setting goals, adopting a growth mindset, seeking feedback, and building a learning community, individuals can pursue lifelong learning effectively and achieve lasting happiness and fulfillment.

36: Conclusion: Putting It All Together - Embracing Contentment for a Fulfilling Life

Throughout this comprehensive self-help guide, we have explored the concept of contentment and its role in achieving lasting happiness. We have delved into the many different facets of contentment, from gratitude and mindfulness to self-compassion and self-care. We have explored the psychological and emotional benefits of contentment, as well as its impact on our physical health and relationships.

At the heart of it all, contentment is about finding peace and fulfillment in the present moment. It's about recognizing that true happiness doesn't come from external sources like money, possessions, or achievements. Rather, it comes from within, from cultivating a sense of gratitude and acceptance for what we have right now, and learning to appreciate the simple pleasures of life.

In this final chapter, we will bring together all the concepts and strategies we have explored throughout this guide and offer practical tips for integrating them into your daily life. Whether you are just starting out on your journey to contentment or are looking to deepen your practice, these tools and techniques will help you embrace contentment and unlock its transformative power in your life.

First and foremost, it's important to remember that contentment is a practice, not a destination. It's something that we need to work on every day, through conscious effort and intention. But with practice and persistence, we can cultivate a deep sense of contentment that will sustain us through life's ups and downs.

One of the most powerful tools for cultivating contentment is gratitude. Taking time each day to reflect on the things we are grateful for can help shift our focus from what we lack to what we have. Whether it's a roof over our heads, a loving relationship, or the beauty of nature, there is always something to be grateful for. You can start a gratitude journal, write thank-you notes to people who have made a difference in your life, or simply take a few moments each day to silently reflect on your blessings.

Mindfulness is another key practice for cultivating contentment. By learning to be fully present in the moment, we can let go of worries about the future and regrets about the past, and appreciate the richness of our experiences right now. Mindfulness can be practiced through formal meditation, but it can also be incorporated into everyday activities like eating, walking, or even brushing your teeth. By paying attention to your senses and your surroundings, you can bring a sense of peace and contentment to even the most mundane tasks.

Self-compassion is also essential for cultivating contentment. We often hold ourselves to impossibly high standards, and beat ourselves up when we fall short. But by learning to treat ourselves with the same kindness and compassion that we offer to others, we can break free from this cycle of self-criticism and find a sense of peace and acceptance. You can practice self-compassion by treating yourself as you would a good friend, acknowledging your feelings without judgment, and offering yourself words of comfort and encouragement.

Self-care is another important aspect of contentment. Taking care of our physical and emotional needs can help us feel more centered and balanced, and better equipped to handle life's challenges. Self-care can take many forms,

from getting enough sleep and exercise to indulging in hobbies and spending time with loved ones. By prioritizing self-
care, we can nourish our bodies and minds, and cultivate a
sense of contentment that comes from feeling healthy and
energized.

Finally, it's important to remember that contentment is not
about giving up on our goals or settling for less than we deserve. Rather, it's about finding joy and fulfillment in the
journey, and recognizing that true happiness comes from
within. By embracing contentment and living in the present
moment, we can unlock the power of this transformative
practice and achieve lasting happiness in all areas of our
lives.

In conclusion, contentment is a powerful tool for achieving
lasting happiness and fulfillment in life. By cultivating gratitude, mindfulness, self-compassion, self-care, and a focus
on the present moment, we can find peace and acceptance
in even the most challenging circumstances.

As you continue on your journey to contentment, remember
that it's a practice that requires ongoing effort and intention. There will be times when you feel discouraged or over-

whelmed, but by staying committed to your practice and seeking support from loved ones or a professional, you can overcome these challenges and find the inner peace and fulfillment you deserve.

Above all, remember that contentment is not something you need to earn or achieve. It's already within you, waiting to be unlocked. By embracing the power of contentment and living in the present moment, you can discover the secrets to a fulfilling life and achieve lasting happiness. So take a deep breath, let go of your worries, and embrace the power of contentment today.

Thank You

As we reach the end of this book, I want to say thanks for reading this book.

I want to get this information out to as many people as possible. If you found this book helpful, I would greatly appreciate you leaving me a review. This helps others find the book as well.

Disclaimer

This document is geared towards providing exact and reliable information in regards to the topic and issue covered. The publication is sold on the idea that the publisher is not required to render an accounting, officially permitted, or otherwise, qualified services. If advice is necessary, legal, financial, medical or professional, a practiced individual in the profession should be ordered.

This information is not presented by a financial or medical practitioner and is for entertainment, educational and informational purposes only. The content is not intended as a substitute for professional medical advice, diagnosis, or treatment. Always seek the advice of your physician or other qualified health care provider with any questions you may have regarding a medical condition. Never disregard professional medical advice or delay in seeking it because of something you have read.

The information provided herein is stated to be truthful and consistent, in that any liability, in terms of inattention or otherwise, by any usage or abuse of any policies, processes, or directions contained within is the solitary and utter responsibility of the recipient reader. Under no circumstances

DISCLAIMER

will any legal responsibility or blame be held against the publisher for any reparation, damages, or monetary loss due to the information herein, either directly or indirectly.